"Dr. Vieira's great strength is that she is so well grounded in theory yet her examples are lively and clear. She makes the most complicated concepts accessible to all of us who need to resolve these core issues."
—Judy LeMaster, Ph.D.. Clinical Psychologist and
Assistant Professor, Scripps College

"This book gives you peace of mind because it presents everything in the context of successful change. You can find where you are in life. Look back and feel exhilarated. Look ahead and see a happier, saner future."
—Nanci Rosen, Marketing Analyst

"I related to so many of your stories and examples. I found myself reflecting on our family life and reviewing the values and beliefs we instill in our son."
—Stacy Kearney, Regional Administration Manager

"I have spent many hours with this work. The ideas are great. It's clear Alice knows this subject well."
—Tom Hubbard, CFS, CFP

"Alice, I learned a lot. The chapters stand alone and the book is fantastic. The map making process at the end, the questions, are easy to understand and use."
—Cathie Sandstrom Smith, Certified Advertising Specialist

"**Belief Systems and Your Personal Power** is terrific and much needed. I could understand and identify with a lot of it. I would love to read it again."
—Linne Weber Malloy, Owner, Westcoast Elevator Pad Company

"This is very good. I've read a lot of the "self-help" books on the market and Alice writes it in a way that is easy to understand."
—Kris Hollowaty, Massage Therapist

"This book makes me think and consider my life in a new light."
—Judith Wilson, Private Pilot

"This book discusses those core issues that shape our personalities and beliefs about ourselves and those people around us. Your quotes are from the authors I enjoyed the most also."
—Helen Temple Bumgardner, R.N.

"You may be jolted by this extraordinary book which invites you to look at reality in a new way and find joy in it. Here is the ultimate guidebook for personal growth and change. You'll treasure Alice's insights on healing and empowerment."
—John F. Thie, D.C., International Touch for Health Lecturer

Belief Systems
and
Your Personal Power

Belief Systems
and
Your Personal Power

What you must know in order to change

Why "self-help" books don't help

Alice Vieira, Ph.D.

Publishers

TPCS books may be purchased for educational and business use. For information please write the address listed above.

Copyright © 1994
First Printing 1994

Advanced Duplicating & Printing
7419 Washington Ave. S.
Edina, MN 55439

Printed in the United States of America

Publisher's Cataloging in Publication
(Prepared by Quality Books Inc.)

Vieira, Alice
    Belief systems and your personal power/Alice Vieira.
    p. cm.
    Includes bibliographical references.
    ISBN 1-88563-404-8

  1. Self-actualization (Psychology) 2. Self-actualization (Psychology)--Case studies. 3. Self-help techniques. I. Title.

BF637.S4V54 1994   158.1
                          QBI94-1394

ISBN 1-88563-404-8 Softcover
94 95 96 97 98 RRD 10 9 8 7 6 5 4 3 2 1

Grateful acknowledgement is made for permission to reproduce the following material: Excerpts from The *Power is Within You* © 1991 by Louise Hay. Behavioral Barometer © reprinted by permission by Gordon Stokes. *PKP-- "Sabotage programs"* © reprinted by permission by Bruce and Joan Dewe. Excerpts from The *Celestine Prophecy* by James Redfield reprinted by permission of Warner Books Inc. Copyright © 1993. *Pathogenic beliefs common to people with substance abuse and dependency problems* from Lynn O'Connor, Ph.D. and Joseph Weiss, M.D. with permission from Lynn O'Connor. Originally published in California Psychologist and Journal of Psychoactive Drugs. Excepts from *"Symbolic Church Fights"* by Nancy Myer Hopkins. Originally printed in Congregations. Excerpts from *Healing the Child Within* by Charles Whitfield. Charts reprinted by permission of Charles Whitfield, Health Communications © 1987. Excerpts from *Toward a Psychology of Being* by Abraham Maslow. Reprinted by permission by Van Nostrand Reinhold. Excerpts from *Group Processes* by Joseph Luft © 1963, 1970 and 1984. Reprinted by permission from Mayfield Publishing Company. Excerpts from *Military Brats* © by Mary Edwards Wertsch. Reprinted by permission from Crown Publishing Group. Excerpts from *Please Understand Me* © 1978 by David Keirsey and Marilyn Bates reprinted by permission by Prometheus Nemesis Book Co. Excerpts from *The Doormat Syndrome* © by Lynne Namka. Reprinted by permission of the author. Excerpt adapted from *Childhood and Society,* Second Edition by Erik H. Erikson, with the permission of W.W. Norton & Company, Inc. Copyright 1950, (c) 1963 by W.W. Norton & Company, Inc. Excerpts from *Homecoming: Reclaiming and Championing Your Inner Child* by John Bradshaw © 1990 by John Bradshaw. Used by permission of Bantam Books, a division of Bantam Doubleday Dell Publishing Group, Inc. Excerpts from *Courage to Heal* by Ellen Bass and Laura Davis. Copyright © 1988 Harper & Row. Excerpts from *Toxic Parents* by Susan Forward. Copyright 1989 by Susan Forward. Used by permission of Bantam Books, a division of Bantam Doubleday Dell Publishing Group, Inc. Excerpts from *Applications of The Seven Habits of Highly Effective People* by Stephen R. Covey. Used by permission of Covey Leadership Center, Inc. 1-800-331-7716. All rights reserved. Excerpts from *On Becoming A Person* by Carl R. Rogers. Copyright © 1961 by Houghton Mifflin Company. Used with permission. Excerpts from *Messages* Copyright © 1983 by Matthew McKay, Martha Davis and Patrick Fanning. Used by permission of New Harbinger Publications.

TABLE OF CONTENTS

FIGURES

DEDICATION

—To my father, John C Thie, who reaches for the highest star.

—To my mother, Mary Butkevich Thie, who believes I can do anything.

—To my brother, John F. Thie, who brags about me.

Also to John Gilfillan, Monty Jones, Warren Jones, David Keirsey, Tom Smith, Fritz Perls, Jim Simkin, Gina Pizzo, Irv Berkowitz, Rose Marie Michelson, John Exner, Sue Colligan, Nancy Haller, John Tulley, Laurel Anderson, Arthur Kovacs, Dan Clifford, Dorothea MacArthur, Larry Hedges, Victor Frank, Gordon Stokes, Bruce Dewe and Joan Dewe, Frank Mahony, Mary Louise Muller, Wayne Topping, Rosmarie Sonderegger Studer, Dominique Monette, and Renate Wennekes whose patience and wisdom I carry with me every day of my life. I heard their words in my head, and I felt their love in my heart as I wrote this book. I am grateful these people were my role models and mentors.

ACKNOWLEDGMENTS

My greatest appreciation goes to artist Kim Vieira who has the ability to condense into a few pen strokes the most complex human emotions and situations with humor and wisdom. During the height of my own involvement with the book, he read it and "sketched" some impressions to "lighten my load." I laughed, and continue to laugh, at his interpretation of these concepts. I am very grateful.

Kim Vieira is also my husband, who, in addition to the artwork, also contributed many months in the publishing, printing, computer consulting, warm hugs, shoulder rubs, balancings, and complete and utter support. No amount of words could express my appreciation, love and devotion.

Thanks to my Touch For Health colleagues who launched this book. A special thank you to John McMullin, without whose continual urging this book would not have been completed. And to Jan Cole and Wayne Topping who gave me confidence to "go ahead and do it."

I would also like to thank the following friends and colleagues for reading drafts of this book and for giving me input, support, and encouragement: Hap and Elizabeth Barhydt, Steve Byrne, Jeff and Helen Bumgardner, Susan Courtney, Carol Cowen, Jeannete Deybrook, Judie Framan, Linda Grinstead, Patti Hayes, Marco Hernandez, Kris Hollowaty, Tom Hubbard, Stacy Kearney, Marvin and Cheri Kliman, Deidre Lisenby, Larry Moore, Linne Weber Malloy, Alison Nathan, Lisa Newell, Susan Platero, Lloyd Priesont, Carole Savola, Julie Sayers, Katherine Schwarzenbach, Malcolm Sherman, Bill Smith, Cathie Sandstrom Smith, Charlie Stavola, John F. Thie Pam and Sam Vickery, Keith Waldon, Gregory Williams, Judith Wilson, Charlotte Winters and Gertie Zint..

I would also like to express my appreciation to Joan Fry, Liz Hargrove, Nanci Rosen, Beth Penney, Tom Hubbard and Jane Stavola for their patience, editing skills and helpful suggestions.

A special thanks to my friends Judy LeMaster, who was there for me at all hours of the day and night to center me in my thinking about the concepts I wanted to use, and John Sawyer, who critiqued my work lovingly.

I especially want to thank my mother, age 86, who read my book many times, checking on typographical errors and passages when "it got too deep." I especially loved the time she read the parts about her and said, "I'm not sure I like that part and I'm so sorry I hurt you. It happened so you have to say it!" Resolution is a wonderful thing!

I am enormously grateful to all my clients and friends who shared with me and have given me permission to use examples of their lives. My work with them brings me incredible joy. Seeing them grow and change as they see fit humbles me and makes me very proud.

Lastly, I want to acknowledge my dear, 11-year-old cat, Minny, who spent the most time with me, on my lap, during the many hours I spent at my desk. Her loving purr kept me grounded, and in touch with the joy I felt writing this book.

Thank you all.

Facilitating change in people has been the driving force throughout my career.

As I moved through the ranks from teacher to high school principal I was fascinated by how students changed. When I referred students to outside agencies I was impressed by the change in behavior of the students who were counselled. When I referred students to Dr. Gilfillan, a psychiatrist, I was impressed that students would "straighten up" and that I, as Dean, would not see them again for problems.

As a result of admiring Dr. Gilfillan's work did, I wrote him a letter asking how I could be on his staff. He took me on as his protege in 1967. Subsequently, I returned to graduate school to become a Clinical Psychologist, then a Touch For Health Instructor and a Professional Kinesiology Practitioner.

I now work with individuals and couples, in private and group settings in private practice. Some people are in therapy with me for a few months; some have been in therapy with me for many years. With all of these clients, my effort is in facilitating change.

The purpose of *Belief Systems and Your Personal Power* is to heighten the awareness of individuals seeking change in their lives. The book examines why some people change, why others stay "stuck" in unhappy or unproductive situations and why some take longer than others to change.

As a clinical psychologist, I am disturbed by the simplicity of most self-help literature. It is unfair to propose that we can "read away" lifelong problems. After twenty-five years of knowing clients who have read virtually every self-help book printed, I have an intense desire to let you in on the truth: *change is not easy.*

The gap between awareness and change lies in our belief systems. It is not easy to stop repeating old, unproductive and painful patterns of living by reading or thinking about failed relationships, poor parenting, sexual abuse, fears, panic, anger, or any unfortunate and thoroughly human conditions.

There is a *huge chasm* between understanding our problems and changing the way we think, feel, and behave. We cannot simply chop the heads off weeds in our garden and expect that a lush green lawn will appear. Weeds and roots can destroy anything in their path. We have to dig out the gnarly roots and weeds, improve the soil and then plant healthy, new seedlings.

How do we make real change? We must uncover our core belief systems and change the limiting and self-defeating ones. These beliefs are formed early and are reinforced over a lifetime of experiences. These belief systems are the reason we act the way we do, and must come into our conscious awareness before we can make progress toward change. Then, we must see that we have a choice about what we believe. With choice comes permission to change.

We can uproot our fundamental beliefs about ourselves, other people, and the world around us. With awareness and the necessary processing of these core beliefs, we can have a much happier, more productive life. Yes, then we can make the changes that, until now, we have only read about in books.

This book is about our belief systems--what they are, where they came from, and how to change them. It's like the starter for yogurt or sourdough bread. In this book we have the beginning of a new way to assess our lives so that it is possible to change.

Alice Vieira, Ph.D.
Newport Beach, California
July, 1994

INTRODUCTION

Overview of Our Developmental Tasks

We are complicated human beings. Knowing how complicated we are and how to uncomplicate ourselves comes through knowledge and awareness. I believe if *we know what is going on, we can change*. When we *don't know that we don't know*, we hold on dearly to what we *do know* because we believe that what we know is all there is. Our growth through the developmental tasks is a series of validations moving toward our individuation. The *self-in-process* serves as an overall center of organization for each of these experiences of validation which allow us to separate and become our own persons.

Table 1

As we grow we either establish a trust in our environment or we do not. This idea is central to this book, so I present the table here for easy reference. As a framework I have used *Erik Erikson's Developmental Stages*.[1] Within the fundamental stages of development I have incorporated the *Sabotage Programs* in Bruce Dewe's Professional Health Provider III Manual [2] and Gordon Stokes' and Daniel Whiteside's *Pain of Life vs. Well-Behaviors*. [3]

Table 1 is only a tool to think with in digging out our core belief systems. It is based on some of Erikson's underlying assumptions about the development of the human being: (1) "We develop according to steps predetermined in our growing readiness to be driven toward, to be aware of, and to interact with, a widening social radius;" and (2) Each critical item of psychosocial strength discussed here is systematically related to all others, and that they all depend on the proper development in the proper sequence of each step." [4]

The task of establishing trust, autonomy, initiative, industry, identity and intimacy can either be accomplished or not. Table 1 list results of a favorable or unfavorable outcome of each.

Table 2 is a summary of Table 1, listing the age of the task, the conflict, the primary relationship focus for that age and the favorable outcome to the resolution of the conflict.

Referring to Table 1 in its entirety or Table 2, for quick reference, will be helpful throughout your reading of this book.

I wish you new awareness!

Table 1

F A V O R A B L E   O U T C O M E S

If *TRUST* IS established, the following feelings result:

OVERALL OPTIMISM, ABILITY TO RELAX, FEELING EQUAL TO ANY
CHALLENGE, DRIVE and HOPE, TIME COMPETENCE

"I have a right to be here, to be taken care of, to feel loved and loveable, to have needs that will be respected and taken care of."

"I can explore, be curious, and experiment in my world. I can do things and get support at the same time. I can get attention and approval and still act the way I really feel without taking you into account."

If *AUTONOMY* IS established, the following feelings result:

OVERALL ADEQUACY, ASSERTIVENESS, SELF-CERTAINTY,
SELF-CONTROL, WILL POWER

"It's OK for me to push my limits, to say NO and to become separate from my parents. I can think for myself. I don't have to take care of others. I can be sure about what I need. I can think about my feelings and I can feel about my thinking. I can let people know when I'm angry. I'm glad to be growing up and separating by having my own feelings."

If *INITIATIVE* IS established, the following feelings result:

CONFIDENCE IN SELF, ABILITY TO DEAL WITH REAL ISSUES, SENSE
OF EQUALITY, PERSONAL SETTING OF PURPOSE AND DIRECTION

"It's OK for me to have my own view of the world, to be who I am and to test my power. It's OK for me to imagine things without being afraid I'll make them come true. I don't have to be scary, sick, sad or mad to be taken care of. I can be powerful and still have needs. It's OK to find out the consequences of my own behavior. It's OK for me to explore who I am. It's important for me to find out what I'm about."

Table 1

UNFAVORABLE OUTCOMES

If *TRUST IS NOT* established, then *MISTRUST IS*, resulting in:

OVERALL PESSIMISM, PREOCCUPATION WITH PAIN, EXPECTATION OF FAILURE, TIME CONFUSION

"I don't ever feel like I belong. My needs are not OK so I cannot share them with you or even myself. I am not a lovable person."

"It's not OK for me to be curious and discover things on my own. I need to wait until you tell me how to feel. When I do things on my own I do not get support. I do not get attention nor approval if I act on my own. I must accept what I am told."

IF AUTONOMY IS NOT established, then *SHAME AND DOUBT ARE*, resulting in:

ANXIETY, DEPRESSION, INDIFFERENCE, SELF-CONSCIOUSNESS, SELF-DOUBT, DENIAL OF PROBLEMS OTHER THAN PAIN

"I do not push and test my limits. I do not say NO directly. It is not OK to be separate from my parents. It is my job to know how others feel and to take care of them first. I cannot feel about my thinking because my feelings are not OK. I cannot think about my feelings because I don't know what they are."

IF INITIATIVE IS NOT established, then *GUILT IS*, resulting in:

DOCTOR SHOPPING, WITHDRAWAL, AVOIDANCE, ESCAPE, GRIEF AND REGRET, ROLE FIXATION

"My view of the world is not important. Who I am is not important. Not making waves is important. I have to be careful about what I think. I have to be scary, sick, sad or mad to be taken care of. I have to be powerful without needs because if I am needy I give up all power. My behavior has bad consequences if I think of myself or my needs. My purpose here is to please others."

Table 1

FAVORABLE OUTCOMES

If *INDUSTRY* IS established, the following feelings result:

PRODUCTIVITY, COMPETENCE, ASSURANCE, ABILITY TO COMMUNICATE FEELINGS AND TO BE DIRECT

"It's OK for me to learn to do things my own way, to have my own morals and methods. I don't have to suffer to get what I need. I can trust my feeling to guide me. I can think before I make something my way. It's OK for me to disagree."

If *IDENTITY* IS established, the following feelings result:

INTEGRATED SELF-IN-PROCESS, HEALTHY SEXUAL IDENTITY FAITH IN RESILIENCY, FAITH IN SEPARATENESS ENTHUSIASM FOR LIFE, DEVOTION AND FIDELITY

"It's OK to be sexual. It's OK for me to be on my own. It's OK for me be to responsible for my own needs, feelings and behaviors. I know my parents send me on the journey of life with their love and support. I know I'm welcome to come home."

If *INTIMACY* IS established, the following feelings result:

ABILITY TO FORM CLOSE PERSONAL RELATIONSHIPS WITH AFFECT-ION AND LOVE, ABILITY TO MAKE A HEALTHY COMMITMENT TO A NOURISHING PERSON, ABILITY TO MAKE A COMMITMENT TO A REWARDING AND SATISFYING CAREER

"I am uniquely myself and honor the uniqueness of others. I continue to expand my commitments. I can be creative, competent, productive and joyful. I trust my inner wisdom. I can finish each part of my journey and look forward to the next. My ability to love matures and expands."

Table 1

U N F A V O R A B L E   O U T C O M E S

IF INDUSTRY IS NOT established, then *INFERIORITY* IS, resulting in:

EXCLUSION FROM SOCIAL CONTACTS, WORK PARALYSIS, USE OF PAIN TO MANIPULATE, CONSTANT FEAR OF LOSS

"The only way I feel OK is if I please someone else or if I suffer. My feelings lead to no good. I am a loner and it is better that way. I must be secretive if I do things my way."

IF IDENTITY IS NOT established, then *ROLE CONFUSION* IS, resulting in:

HOSTILITY, WITHDRAWAL FROM ACTIVE SEX LIFE, PAIN IS AN ADDICTION, SENSE OF FUTILITY

"Sex doesn't seem right for me. I have a low sex drive. When I am sexual it is for my partner's pleasure. Exceeding my parents (happiness, career, yearly income, etc.) might hurt them, so I must be careful to monitor my successes. The validity of my feelings and thinking depends on your reaction. If I leave you it will not be with your blessing and I will not be welcome to return home."

IF INTIMACY IS NOT established, then *ISOLATION* IS, resulting in:

INCREASING INCIDENTS OF DEPRESSION, ANXIETY, RESENTMENT, IDENTIFICATION WITH OTHERS SUFFERING, INCREASING RESTRICTIONS DUE TO FEAR OF MORE PAIN

"I do not make commitments. I struggle with my career and have not found a direction. I am rigid. I have a hard time finishing things. I am not lovable unless I please someone. My needs are not important. I am not important."

Table 2

AGE	CONFLICT	SOCIAL FOCUS	FAVORABLE OUTCOME
Birth-18 mon	TRUST or MISTRUST	PRIMARY CARETAKERS	DRIVE and HOPE
18 mon-3 yrs	AUTONOMY or SHAME and DOUBT	PARENTS	SELF-CONTROL and WILL POWER
3-6 yrs	INITIATIVE or GUILT	BASIC FAMILY	DIRECTION and PURPOSE
6-11 yrs	INDUSTRY or INFERIORITY	SCHOOL and NEIGHBORHOOD	METHOD and COMPETENCE
12-18 yrs	IDENTITY or ROLE CONFUSION	PEERS/ROLE-MODELS/MENTORS	DEVOTION and FIDELITY
Early Adulthood	INTIMACY or ISOLATION	PARTNERS/LOVERS/MATES	AFFECTION and LOVE

"Think of this:
If you accept full responsibility for your life
then you will accept that your destiny is created by you
and that your life is basically a symbol of your
innermost thoughts and feelings--
what you believe about yourself."
—Stuart Wilde

"Inherently, each one of us has the substance within to
achieve whatever our goals and dreams define.
What is missing from each of us
is the training, education, knowledge and insight
to utilize what we already have."
—Mark Twain

IS THERE A WAY TO CHANGE?

"Grow in any direction and
joy as well as pain will be your reward.
The only alternative is not to live fully or
not to live at all."
—M. Scott Peck

"A mind stretched to a new idea
never returns
to its original dimension."
—Oliver Wendell Holmes

Our conscious awareness of an old idea *as* an old idea is essential for change. To stretch our minds to accept a new idea, we must be willing to go beyond our automatic behavior and change our thinking. We must grasp the *reality* of how difficult it is to change. Why?

We utilize only two to three percent of our brain's capability. Wayne Dyer, a leader in the field of self-development, says that who we are and what we are is only about one percent of what we can see, touch or feel. We are not our faces or hands or brains. Who we are has to do with how we feel and what we think. We can actually change our body chemistry by our thoughts. ₅ Because we use only a small percentage of our brain potential, and because we are so much more than what we manifest physically, isn't it shocking that we so vigorously defend behavior, which, for the most part, is beyond our awareness?

GETTING THROUGH THE UNAWARENESS

On the wall of my office, I have posted three sayings that I have heard at conferences over the years:

We cannot talk ourselves out of anything we have behaved into.

No healing can take place without expansion of consciousness.

If something conflicts with existing belief systems, it will not be integrated.

The unresolved and unrecognized issues that form some of our belief systems direct our actions automatically. The problem is, we need to be motivated to move through unawareness and behavior that is automatic, so that those issues will not continue to direct our actions as they have in the past--over and over again.

Paula Oleska, in her paper, *Emotional Integration,* states that: "Over 148,000 negative commands (and very few positive ones) are given to us by the time we are 18 years old." Imagine the belief systems that are built as a result of these 148,000 messages! [6] Because we desperately want to please our parents, the magical connections between what is heard and what becomes our automatic behavior become very difficult to dig out.

M. Scott Peck begins his book, *The Road Less Traveled*, with the sentence, "Life is difficult." [7] The point of the chapter is that, once we realize life is difficult, the rest is easy. If we fight the reality that life is difficult, then the rest is impossible, for we will always struggle. This is my point as well. Everything we do comes from of a set of beliefs. The limiting or self-defeating belief systems of which we are unaware are the ones I want to address.

Wayne Topping, in his book, *What Makes You Tick, Makes You Sick,* defines a limiting belief as one that causes anxiety when it is not adhered to;

4

that limiting belief activates negative emotions and throws our internal organs out of balance. [8]

Jeffery Pease defines a self-defeating belief system as (1) one that makes you feel some way that you don't like feeling; (2) one that is not true; and (3) one that crushes life rather than enhances it, cutting you off from what you want most. [9]

When we grasp the idea that digging out our core belief systems and turning from unawareness to awareness is very difficult, the journey can be rewarding. When we defend a limiting or self-defeating belief, we lessen our capacity to grow.

We *can* go beyond our belief system. We *can* grow toward our potential and never return to our old beliefs in the same way. Frederick Perls, the father of Gestalt therapy, said, "If we spit in our soup, it never tastes quite the same way again." [10]

"You spit in my soup!"

What we believe and act upon is what we believe deep inside our beings. What makes believing what we believe even more complicated, is that what we believe to be true now *was true* for us at one time in our lives. We needed diapers at one time and that belief was based in reality. If, however, we still believe we need diapers, we are acting on *old, un-useful beliefs*, and we need to have someone "spit in our soup."

We need to know what our core belief systems are before we can alter them. Without this knowledge, we cannot identify limiting beliefs; without identifying them, there will be no change.

There is a movement for short-term intervention in the field of psychology. There are clinics where clients are expected to change in six sessions. One of my clients reported that during the first of six sessions he was given an assignment to complete before the second session could be scheduled. The assignment was an extensive series of written exercises geared toward making him aware of what he was doing in relationships, thoughts and actions. Even though the client had paid in advance for the six sessions, he did not complete the exercises; therefore, he did not return. His substantial financial investment, combined with the goal of a quick remedy, was not enough to create awareness and change.

It is *not* easy to change! The things that we want to change, that we feel need to be changed, involve more than the decision to be different. There is a reason we develop the habits and ways of being.

Self-help books continue to top the bestseller lists, but psychologists still make a good living. If just reading about change could make a lasting difference, libraries and bookstores would put practitioners out of business. Somewhat self-consciously, I feel compelled to state my utter frustration at the number of self-help books on shelves everywhere. Most of my clients have a self-help book collection bigger than my lending library. The problem is that self-help books encourage a *voyeuristic approach* to change; people can get involved in how interesting change might be. But that is a false sense of direction. Many people read a book and decide they will change. But, unfortunately, that commitment is like a New Year's resolution. Changing is simply not that easy.

For the most part, the self-help movement is merely a small band-aid on life-threatening wounds. Psychological wounds need diagnosis, awareness, intervention, and practice because core belief systems are imprinted in our beings.

Therapist's dream

I myself have changed, therefore I know change is possible. I have been privileged to work with many people who have changed, and with many people who have not changed. We are all doing the very best that we can to live our lives--just as our parents, and their parents did before them. But the "best that we can" may, in some cases, not be enough to alter the automatic behavior that we have adopted in order to feel a measure of safety.

There are thousands of self-help books on how to change. This book is not on *how to change,* but rather on *how to become aware of what to change,* should we choose to do so. My purpose is to suggest ways to gain insight into our vast area of unawareness. We cannot change what is unconscious. Changing cannot take place without opening up and expanding conscious awareness!

WHAT ARE CORE BELIEFS?

The first step to understanding core beliefs is to know the automatic behavior that stems from words that we heard, believed and acted into our lives *as if* they were true forever. The following is a partial list of beliefs that I hear from people seeking help. Are any of these beliefs true for you?

Living Core Beliefs

☐   If I'm a good girl/boy, good things will happen to me.

☐   Life is fair.

☐   If I am honest, I will get hurt.

☐   There is always tomorrow.

☐   "To thine own self be true" means not to listen to anyone else.

☐   I will be taken care of.

☐   The world will change for me.

☐ Anger is bad.

☐ Anger hurts people.

☐ If I'm angry, I am bad.

☐ I can't know what I want.

☐ If I get my needs met, it is at your expense.

☐ If I do what you say, I will lose control of me.

☐ I shouldn't feel this way.

☐ I should be better than I am now.

☐ Life should be a bowl of cherries.

☐ If I tell you what I want, you won't give it to me.

☐ Be careful what you ask for, you might get it.

☐ If I state my needs, I am selfish.

☐ If I don't feel bad, I won't keep trying.

☐ If I fail, everyone will know and hate me for it.

☐ Saying how I feel about my parents is betraying them.

☐ I have to grin and bear it.

☐ I have to pay my dues.

☐ I can't expect to be happy all the time.

☐ Life has its ups and downs.

☐ My mother loves me.

☐ My father is always right.

☐ Since I am not pleasing my mother/father, I am bad.

☐ Going to bed early will make me healthy, wealthy and wise.

☐ If you know me, you will hate me.

☐ Victims are not to blame.

☐ What I think is wrong.

☐ If I am all I can be, you won't like me.

☐ Anxiety stops me from functioning.

☐ Anxiety means I'm about to lose total control.

☐ Love is everything.

☐ I'll never amount to anything.

☐ I have enough intelligence but not enough self-discipline.

INTERPRETING YOUR BELIEFS

When we examine our belief systems, our perception about the facts and how we feel about them can change. The following statements show beliefs changed for some of my clients after exploring their real circumstances.

Beliefs versus Reality

Beliefs/Myths	Reality
I was daddy's special girl.	My father molested me.
Father knows best.	He was wrong.
He did the best he could.	Ignorance is no excuse.
My mom had it rough.	My mom is very selfish.
We had the perfect family.	Our family is dysfunctional.

I was a rough kid. I deserved it.	I was a kid. No kid deserves to be whipped.
It wasn't their fault.	It was their responsibility.
My parents love me.	My parents love themselves.
I'm bad.	Kids aren't bad.
If I don't appreciate them, I'm bad.	Kids aren't bad. My feelings are OK.
If I'm criticized, I'm nothing.	Criticism is something to be considered.
Criticism is devastating.	Criticism is someone's opinion, nothing more.
I must please my parents.	I must be me regardless of pleasing my parents.

THE POWER OF LIVING WITH YOUR PERSONAL TRUTHS

We have to recognize that living in the present is primary. We have to recognize the way we relate and the roles we play now. To get beyond the roles, one client began to recognize family (tribal) beliefs that had been acted upon from generation to generation but now were contrary to his personal beliefs and goals. This realization was his first step in getting beyond the roles he played. He developed the following list to contrast his beliefs with those of his parents and grandparents.

12

TRIBAL MYTHS VERSUS PERSONAL GOALS

Family/Tribal Beliefs

Personal Beliefs and Goals

1. Physical bodies should be indestructible; they should absorb abuse without complaint and without maintenance.

1. I am grateful that I have a strong, healthy body. I know that health is fragile, and I care for my body with good nutrition and regular exercise.

2. When we are sick, others should take care of us, feel sorry for us, and not expect anything of us.

2. When I am sick, I do not request or expect special treatment. I take responsibility for co-operating with nature in restoring myself to good health.

3. We know what's best for us.

3. I benefit from the input and feedback of others who can be more objective about my situation than I can.

4. We don't need other people; we have casual relationships but very few friends.

4. I am grateful for friends who share intimately with me.

5. Men keep things to themselves.

5. Men and women who are open and direct benefit from enhanced communication and improved mental health.

6. Men make the financial decisions.

6. Spouses share financial information openly with each other and negotiate decision-making.

7. We don't think or talk about emotions. We block them completely out of awareness.

7. I am fully aware of my emotions and express them freely.

8. We are "private" people. We don't need to make a public display of ourselves. We don't stand in front of people and talk about ourselves.

8. I talk openly about my life in appropriate situations.

9. We have a valuable commodity, things others want. People come to us, we do not go to them. Our strength is in our reputation for quality.

9. I have valuable information and products to offer, and it is my obligation to make sure that others have the opportunity to consider and benefit from them.

10. We insulate ourselves from unpleasantness. We do not think about society's problems.

10. I am but one person among five billion on the planet; the needs and aspirations of all the others have a direct effect on me.

11. Life should be smooth and easy. "The world owes us a living!"

11. Life is challenging, and I strive to rise to the challenge. I cannot impact everyone else by my decisions and actions, but I can impact those in my "circle of influence," and I am determined to do so in a constructive manner. The weight of my opinions and actions is limited, but I exercise the choice of where and how it will be felt.

12. Any minor inconvenience is a challenge to the prior belief, and must be regarded not only as a personal affront but an attack on universal axioms; therefore any stress or frustration properly calls forth a major reaction: We cannot/will not tolerate this! When one of our number (typically a man) exercises this belief by a noisy or violent reaction, we "freeze" for a moment, then continue as though nothing had happened.

12. The inconveniences and frustrations I experience are generally quite minor. I view them as tiny specks in comparison with the marvelous gift of life.

13. Above all, we should be comfortable!

13. Above all, I will be loving!

BELIEFS ABOUT CHEMICAL DEPENDENCY

Persons who are chemically-dependent hold particular beliefs about their dependency. [11] Chemically-dependent persons believe that in giving up the dependency they would:

☐   Betray a parent.

☐   Betray a family "secret."

☐   Sever an attachment to parents or other loved ones.

☐   Make another family member or members feel inadequate and inferior, and thus cause unhappiness to others.

☐   Outdo a parent or sibling.

☐   Contradict parents' opinions about being bad, destructive or crazy.

☐   Be too forceful and overpower and hurt others.

☐   Continue to cause others to drink, take drugs, overeat, be depressed or violent.

The chemically-dependent person also believes that:

☐   The punishments and/or neglect he or she received as a child were appropriate and deserved.

☐ The loneliness and feelings of being disconnected from family members experienced in childhood were caused by of some inherent personality defect.

☐ His or her need to feel intimately connected to others expresses some excessive need and constitutes a danger to others. He or she does not deserve to be connected.

CHAPTER 2

THE QUESTION OF CHOICE

"Decide what you want,
decide what you are willing to exchange for it.
Establish your priorities and go to work."
—H.L. Hunt

"If there are two courses of action--
you should always take the third."
—Jewish Proverb

"In shamanic societies, weak-heartedness is
when individuals lack the courage
to be authentic.
Strong-heartedness is when we have
the courage to be
who we are in our life."
—Angeles Arrien

"Come on everybody, choose to be happy!"

The question of whether of not we are at choice to change depends on a number of factors. I become irate when I hear a person advise someone else to *choose to change, choose not to be depressed, increase self-esteem,* or *forgive and forget.* If it were that easy, I would be in another profession, because there would be no need for psychologists.

If we believe changing is simply a matter of choice then we can easily fall

Meredith had been diagnosed with cancer. Concomitantly we were working on how she had learned from her parents to be manipulative. The manipulation was now hurting her marriage. I suggested she consider looking at the possible emotional component that Louise Hay suggests in her book *Heal Your Body*. Hay states that the probable emotional cause of cancer is "deep hurt, longstanding resentment, a deep secret or grief eating away at the self, carrying hatreds or thinking 'what's the use?'" [12]

Meredith felt I was blaming her for having cancer. She later lied that she had been "misdiagnosed," because she didn't want to feel that having cancer was her fault.

A friend of mine Jan Cole, had been accused by religious fundamentalists of being a "witch" because, as a public school teacher, she touched the foreheads of her students in order to release emotional stress (a common self-help technique). In discussing her subsequent court battle she was asked by well-meaning colleagues why she was bringing this negative energy to herself, as if the difficulties had been her choice.

The concept of choice should *not be a weapon*. Each particular situation needs to be considered on its own merit. Choice is an option only when we know what our options are.

Nancy Joekel, one of the first faculty members in Touch For Health, spoke on *The Question of Choice*. I agreed with Nancy's view that it is cavalier to assert that someone can choose to be happy, choose not to be depressed, or choose to have different circumstances. She likened these choices to choosing whether or not to sweat. Obviously, not everything is merely a question of choice. [13]

Do we have a choice when we are under a great deal of stress? Do we have a choice when we are trying to survive? How early in life do we have choice? When does choice become part of our repertoire? At what stage in our development is choice a question?

Figure 1
Maslow's Hierarchy of Needs

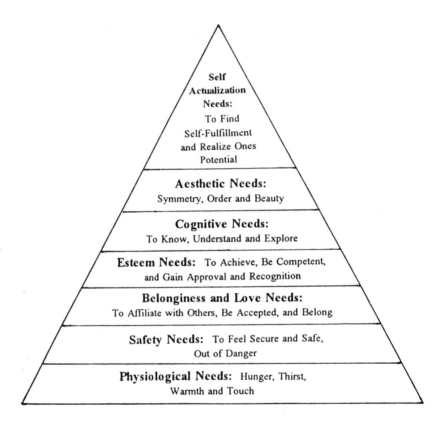

Self Actualization Needs: To Find Self-Fulfillment and Realize Ones Potential

Aesthetic Needs: Symmetry, Order and Beauty

Cognitive Needs: To Know, Understand and Explore

Esteem Needs: To Achieve, Be Competent, and Gain Approval and Recognition

Belonginess and Love Needs: To Affiliate with Others, Be Accepted, and Belong

Safety Needs: To Feel Secure and Safe, Out of Danger

Physiological Needs: Hunger, Thirst, Warmth and Touch

NEEDS ARE HIERARCHICAL

Abraham Maslow proposed an interesting way of looking at the choices we are able to make in relation to the opportunities life offers us. Maslow found that there were two levels of needs, deficiency needs--ones that must be met before any possibility of transcending them can be hoped for--and growth needs--ones that motivate us toward self-fulfillment and realization of one's potential. The needs are hierarchical (Figure 1) ranging from basic survival requirements (food, water, shelter) to the quest for self-actualization. The deficiency needs induce behavior aimed at supplying deficiencies, most of which are available through other people. Without the satisfaction of the needs for survival, being loved, feeling like we belong, we are not at choice to feel confident in the world or with ourselves. The higher needs cannot be satisfied until the lower, more basic needs are satisfied. The needs at the lower end of the hierarchy focus on survival and offer few choices other than alleviating the deficiency. Maslow thought that a fully-functioning person (self-in-process) requires the gratification of all the hierarchical needs.

If we meet our lower biological needs by growing up in a healthy, happy environment, then we are not limited by fears and anxieties, then we can seek to experience life with excitement, spontaneity, and humor. We can be open to new experiences and look to the beauty of the world. 14

We are given an enormous task, as children, to meet the demands of life. Our first task is to survive. Survival needs include getting fed, staying warm and dry, being touched, and being held. The next need is that of safety and a primary sense of security. When we cry or feel fear, we need to be held and reassured.

The next set of needs are those of love and affection. It is important to love and be loved by others and have our feelings validated. Self-esteem follows feeling safe, loved, and sensing we belong. When we have self-esteem, we can take full responsibility for ourselves. If we don't feel loved, accepted and worthy, then we cannot *chose to feel good* about ourselves. Thwarting of our basic needs leads to an endless search for their satisfaction, during which time we are not at choice to reach beyond.

> Jack, a 64-year-old virgin, began dating at age 59. It was ten years after his mother died that he met a woman in her early sixties who was kind and gentle with his inexperience. She understood that she would have to "walk him through" any intimacy there would be in their relationship. Jack was satisfied just to have a companion, although he stated he wanted to have sex at some point in his life. When she proposed a physical relationship he became extremely uncomfortable,

developed migraine headaches and chest pains which the doctor diagnosed as anxiety attacks. Jack worried about everything including whether he would be upset by her body, if he could get or maintain an erection, if she would laugh at him and so on. The dread and apprehension became so great that he ended the relationship before a physical relationship ensued. As soon as he ended the relationship the headaches ceased and so did the chest pain, worry, dread, and apprehension. He survived and felt safe when he did not have the pressure of going further than he could handle.

Until his mother died, Jack had spent his life surviving an unfortunate childhood and over-attachment to his mother. He did not have a sense of belonging because he still did not feel secure and safe in the world. He could not proceed to a level of involvement greater than the needs he had satisfied to date.

Dr. Harold F. Searles, one of the leading psychiatrists in the newest research in psychology of lower-functioning persons, wrote about the issue of choice for psychotics. He suggests that chronic psychosis may be the only subjectively autonomous mode of existence available to a psychotic person. His point is that, for a mentally-ill person even to consider mental health, he/she must feel in a position to choose between continuing insanity on one hand and interpersonal relationships on the other. 15

Choosing to be self-actualized is not a question of choice if we are focused on where we will get our next meal, or whether or not, as children, we will be safe from parental attack or left alone. Before we can decide to change, we need to feel that we are safe, that we belong and that we are loved--then we have freedom to choose.

K. VIEIRA

Shadow of a doubt

What we chose, once we have the choice to chose, depends on our core belief systems about our right to be happy, to feel good about ourselves, to be successful and so on.

Knowing we have choice is crucial to all growth and change. Awareness of the underlying building blocks and faulty foundations in our lives allows us to choose between continued dysfunction and healthy intrapersonal/interpersonal relatedness. For us to become able to choose, we must know, beyond a shadow of a doubt, that we have the choice *not* to change. And we must know the consequences of choosing to remain the same.

"Ma'am, we have a report that there is toxic shame here!"

TOXIC SHAME ALTERS BRAIN CHEMISTRY

Discovering our belief systems and where they came from, and discriminating between our healthy and unhealthy (limiting or self-defeating) belief systems is the only way to change.

John Bradshaw, author and lecturer, describes how toxic shame is imprinted on us. He believes that catastrophic events can alter our brain chemistry. When our parents have their "bad days" and deal with us inappropriately, their worst behavior is imprinted on us at the moment of our greatest vulnerability. It is when our parents are out of control or having their "bad days" that we feel the most threatened. Once our brain chemistry is altered, we become hyper-vigilant and lose touch with necessary internal cues. [16] The anger and pain agitate us repeatedly unless we seek and find resolution. Emotionally we remain traumatized. What we didn't get as children leaves us feeling worthless to our core. Until we do our original pain work, we are not "at choice." We are not able to *choose*.

THE NECESSITY OF OPTIONS

Choice comes from having options. If we are hungry or scared we have fewer options. The way we walk or talk or breathe is not a matter of choice until we become consciously aware of these processes. We can choose to alter, control, or continue those processes of which we have become aware.

One of my clients who had been molested by her father described her fears about not being able to change:

"That child-baby part of me yearns (as part of a fantasy bond, attachment, hunger) for the original abusive, dysfunctional man, sucking his penis instead of mother's breast. I feel another layer of the onion peeling off with accompanying tears. I am staring at those old, petrified,

26

encrusted, hardened layers entombed in the brain cells, the very essence of life, the molecules in the body. Can I change?

Much of the time I live on a new level--happy--playing golf, meditating, talking with people, enjoying my work and life. But underneath the frightened little baby girl lurks, wanting to grab that fleeting, furtive, fucking penis. She says, "Fill me with that milkless semen. Hold my hand and stroke my hair." The baby connects, bonds to its convoluted source of life, feeling dead at the hidden core of nothing-- the black hole. Then the adult brain evaluates what the old brain predictably repeats for survival. Is this repetition compulsion? Is the old brain the sick mind? Is the rat going down the same path again and again and never finding cheese at the end? The old brain rules the lover's path once again to wound the baby's injured soul. The baby knows only what a baby can know...one thing. And in endless repetition she, like the rat, lives in that one lone circle of energy, pathetically pressing the empty button for the non-existent pellet....That center is one millionth, one trillionth of all that is me, but its power in and over me has been limitless. Stop the camera! Reverse? There! That little speck. That's the problem. It yearns. It's very alive. It pulsates like a one-cell organism."

What happened to this client will always be part of her history and, as a result of that history, she will have a different sort of scar from others who have a different history. She will have *no choice* about having been scarred by the sexual abuse. She *will* have choices about how to handle it and resolve the issues surrounding it. Her therapy will consist of resolving the issues with her father so that she can move on with her life.

Ellen Bass and Laura Davis in *Courage To Heal*, describe, in wonderful detail, the process of this resolution:

1. Decide to see the problem for what it is--become aware.

2. Allow yourself to remember what happened.

3. Believe that what you remember did, indeed, happen.

4. Break the silence. Refuse to keep what happened to you a secret.

5. Understand it wasn't your fault.

6. Trust yourself to go through the resolution.

7. Grieve and mourn what wasn't a result of the abuse.

8. Allow the anger--the backbone of your healing.

9. Confront the abuser.

10. Forgive only after the resolution--not before.

11. Recognize a power greater than yourself is there for you.

12. Come to a place of choice where you can choose where to go from here.

13. Decide to heal by taking on what is unfamiliar to you now. 17

    The purpose of this book is to assure you that choosing to change is possible. It is not, however, a *simple matter* of choice. We do the best we can in our lifetime. When we were babies, we were treated in ways that developed our perceptions of how we see the world. We are who we are because of those perceptions. To undo those perceptions (*to change*) we must know from whence those perceptions came. This search requires more than just *choosing change*.

CHAPTER 3

CHANGE
WHY SOME DO
AND OTHERS DON'T

"If you always do what you've always done,
you'll always get what you've always gotten."
— Anon.

"The human race, to which so many of my readers belong,
has been playing at children's games from the beginning,
which is a nuisance for the few who grow up."
—G.K. Chesterton

"If you sow a thought, you reap an action;
If you sow an action, you reap a habit;
If you sow an habit, you reap a character;
If you sow a character, you reap a destiny."
—Kenton Beshore

"We can change.
We can be different.
We can defy history.
We do it by changing the judgments which limit
our thinking and what we try to accomplish."
—Barry Neil Kaufman

What constitutes change? When can we say we have "changed"? Is it when we act a different way or feel differently? Are acting and feeling both necessary for change? Is change really possible? Can we change ourselves by using affirmations? Can we change anyone else? Is change simply an evolution over which we have no control? Is change the same as growth? If we rearrange our priorities, will change happen automatically? Is knowledge change? If we stop habits such as drinking or smoking, will we change? Does change have to be visible for it to be considered change? Does commitment or involvement in something or someone new constitute a change? This chapter attempts to answer some of these questions.

INVOLVEMENT VERSUS COMMITMENT

I once heard an analogy that illustrates the difference between involvement and commitment. Think about bacon and eggs: To produce the eggs, the chicken is involved. To produce the bacon, the pig is committed. Was the chicken changed as a result of the involvement? The pig clearly was!

Involvement is not enough to produce change because change takes more than willingness. There must be a *determination to act, to risk, to be uncomfortable* with what will certainly be unfamiliar. Involvement is a step toward change, because without our involvement, change will not happen. But because of the way we are formed, involvement is only the first step. *Commitment is necessary for change to take place.* Bookstores are filled with self-help books for people who want better lives for themselves, but few will commit themselves to follow what the self-help books advise to accomplish change. The missing piece in this puzzle is the "why,"--why don't we commit to going ahead and committing ourselves to change?

THEORIES ABOUT CHANGING

Before we delve into identifying this missing piece, I want to simplify and summarize some of the theories about change. In theoretical and practical psychology, there are many differing ideas about change. Behavior modificationists believe that positive reinforcements enable change to occur. Gestalt therapists believe that change comes from awareness. Rational emotive therapists believe that change comes from changing how we think about an event, which changes how we feel about the event. Psychoanalysts believe that change comes from insight and from working through the interpretation of the

31

insight. Rogerians believe that change comes when we feel genuinely regarded and validated for our feelings. Object relations theorists believe that change comes from a new quality of relatedness.

Many theorists believe that self-acceptance is a precondition of change. Erik Erikson, an authority on the explanation and clarification of developmental tasks in their various stages, said that it takes a well-established identity to tolerate change. [18] D.W. Winnicott, an expert in the field of child development, said that the only "cure" for adolescence is the time it takes to go from childhood to adulthood, from dependence to independence. [19] William Glasser, the author of *Reality Therapy* said that, if you want to change you have to behave as if you have already changed, focusing on what is right, real, and responsible. [20]

One thing that seems consistent among all the theories is that *change is stressful,* even when the changes are good changes. As, human beings, we prefer being and doing what we have been or have done before. We like to know what to expect, and to seek what gives us a sense of security. Sadly, what is safe and secure is also often static and limiting!

> I recall vividly the change made by a client whom I was treating for depression: After the depression had lifted she told me she missed being depressed. She said that she knew what "being depressed" was like, and that felt more secure than the newness of not being depressed.

> A man I worked with always complained about his lunch. Day after day he would open his brown bag and say, "Oh no, tuna again!" Tired of hearing this, I suggested that he tell his wife to fix him another kind of sandwich. He said, "What do you mean? I fix my own lunches!"

We all fix our own lunches to some degree and often-times we keep fixing tuna!

FREEDOM AS THE POSSIBILITY OF CHANGE

Rollo May, in his book, *Freedom and Destiny*, defines freedom as the possibility of changing. He says that freedom is the ability to change the nature of your being and to become something different from what you were before. He further defines freedom as the possibility of enhancing one's life, but also the possibility of withdrawing, shutting one's self off, denying and stultifying one's growth. If we are free to change, then we must be free *not* to change. Freedom, by its very nature, is the ability to choose. Not being able to change because we do not know how, because we are not aware of the options we have to be different, or are afraid of the unknown, means we are *not free to change*. The freedom to change only comes from the ability to make the choice not to change. If we do not change because of the anxiety the change would cause, then we are not free. [21]

Victor Frankl described the difference between liberty and freedom as a result of his concentration camp experiences in World War II. He states that freedom was the ability to think his own thoughts. Liberty was the ability to move about freely where he wanted to go. Dr. Frankl's captors could not take away his freedom, but they did confiscate his liberty. [22]

Stewart Emery (*Actualizations: You Don't Have to Rehearse to Be Yourself*) and Wayne Dyer (*You Have to Believe It To See It*) use the word "transformation" in the way that I would like to define "change." [23]

Emery said, "If you took an apple and turned it into an orange, that would be a change. But, if you took an apple and turned it into an apple that tasted like an orange, that would be transformation, because it would have the form of an apple and the essence of an orange. If we undergo a transformation, the world and the circumstances in which we find ourselves may be the same. What is altered is the way we feel about and react to the circumstance and the world. What is altered is *our relationship* to the *things* in our life, not the things *in our life*." [24]

One of my clients described life as a great peanut field with weeds, pests, rocks, and boulders in it. To reap a harvest, we must properly tend the peanut field. But no matter how much we read, talk, and think about the number of weeds, the size of rocks and boulders, and the proliferation of pests, the peanut field will not change. What will make the difference between a peanut harvest and no peanut harvest is our commitment to pull the weeds, get rid of the pests, and move the obstacles so that the peanuts will grow. *Buying* the tools does not make the difference. *Knowing which tools will work* and using them will.

There is a quip I enjoy when I think about change:

FEW MAKE THINGS HAPPEN
MANY WATCH THINGS HAPPEN
MOST HAVE NO IDEA WHAT HAPPENED

The following chapters are dedicated to describing what people do in their lives to make things happen so that they have the option to change; removing the fear of the unknown so that the many who watch things happen can do something about them; and convincing those who have no idea what has happened that something is happening so that they can become participants!

A client of mine who was just finishing her psychotherapy wrote the following in 1993 and gave me permission to share it in this book:

I was not in the picture. I lived my life according to what other people-any other people, but particularly my family--wanted to do or where they wanted to go. I sometimes still do that--go along with the crowd or do something that I would rather not do, but now I know when I'm doing it and that it's OK if it doesn't feel right. Mostly, though, I've learned that I do have a right to my opinions and wishes, and that when I make them known, usually it works out. If it doesn't work out exactly the way I pictured it, I know there is room for compromise and flexibility. There

34

are very few issues that are totally black or white, and my input is not only allowed, but valuable.

I've learned to be selfish--learned to say "No," that it's OK to do something that's fun, only for me, even if it means I'm not available for everyone else's needs all the time. In fact, now I believe that my changes have shown my daughter in a very positive way that there is a better way to be a Mom. Putting myself more in the picture shows her that it's OK, and it will be easier for her to value herself and her ideas and needs.

Being in group has given me a place to practice new skills and try out new ideas. I have been unperfect and had unpopular opinions that I was able to express and even be criticized for, and we all lived.

The lessons I've learned and the skills I've developed are not always automatic. I spent many years thinking in unhealthy ways about my rights. But it feels better to matter -- to have a vote. Now that I know and understand that and have experienced the benefits of feeling important, I feel certain I could never go back to the old way of thinking. I like being positive and looking for the best in everyone I meet. I cherish that part of me. Yet I know I need to feel and express negative feelings, because we are all made of both positive and negative feelings and suppressing negative feelings and thoughts is destructive and unhealthy. I'm speaking out more and more and I feel I can continue to do it.

CHANGE

K. VIEIRA

BARRIERS TO CHANGE

BELIEF SYSTEMS
WHAT THEY ARE
AND WHAT THEY DETERMINE

"Reality is what we take to be true.
What we take to be true is what we believe.
What we believe is based on our perceptions.
What we perceive is based on what we look for.
What we look for depends on what we think.
What we think depends on what we perceive.
What we perceive determines what we believe.
What we believe determines what we take to be true.
What we take to be true is our reality."
—Gary Zukav

"Memory believes before knowing remembers."
—William Faulkner

"What lies behind us and what lies before us
are tiny matters compared to what lies within us."
—Ralph Waldo Emerson

A belief system is a deeply-ingrained format that affects the path of our lives. A man who never quite makes it in business may have been imprinted early in life with the belief that he "will never amount to anything." A woman who never wears makeup or dresses up may have been imprinted with the belief that she "is plain and unattractive." Whatever a belief is about will affect what we see, hear, think, judge and perceive. The belief determines the way we live. Attitudes about our belief systems determine what kinds of illnesses we develop and whether or not we survive them. Whatever the belief system has come to be, it is very difficult to change. If we do not address our underlying belief systems, there is a small probability that we will change.

WHERE OUR BELIEF SYSTEMS COME FROM

Belief systems are reflected in our memories, language, emotions, thinking, and behavior. Belief systems are formed early in life by how others treat us, how we see people treat each other, and how others respond to our needs as we grow. They are formed by our surroundings, what we discover intellectually, by our experiences, hopes and expectations. Our belief systems permeates all that we do, how we interact with others, how we handle our feelings and how we give and receive love. Our belief systems are the sum of our assumptions, judgments, myths, and behavior patterns. Our belief systems contain all our family messages about our personal value and worth. They determine how we plan and make decisions, how we interpret other people's actions, how we make meaning out of any experience we have, how we solve problems, how we form relationships, how we develop our careers, and how we establish our priorities. Our belief systems form the filter through which we conduct the business of our lives.

"BELIEVING IS SEEING"

Our senses and intuition are filtered through beliefs. A belief system is a direction: If we don't believe something, we don't put energy into it. To maintain a sense of self, we amend our beliefs and distort reality to suit our beliefs. We add to our beliefs, take away from them, or distort input in order to maintain who we are. If we were wounded in some manner as children, or if we have not separated from our parents or addressed issues with them, our view of the world will be skewed and distorted, but we do not know it. The phrase "seeing is believing" is more accurately stated in the reverse. "Believing is seeing." Wayne Dyer says, "I'll see it when I believe it." What we believe becomes the lens through which we see our world.

Whether we are happy or miserable depends completely on our core belief systems. Milton Erikson, a famous hypnotherapist, states that every person has a unique map of the world, an inner belief system that is unconscious. M. Scott Peck, author of *The Road Less Travelled* (1978) says that mental health is based on two things: the belief in a power greater than ourselves, and the constant struggle to know and be in touch with reality. [25] Isn't it crucial that we examine the nature of the reality in which we believe? Our reality is totally defined by our belief systems; most of our belief systems are unconscious, yet rule everything we do.

Sir John Eccles, a Nobel laureate in neurophysiology, has commented recently on how "extraordinary" the new knowledge of how we think changes the very basic structure of our physical beings. [26]

Blair Justice, in his book *Who Gets Sick* (1988), states:

> Despite this growing evidence, there are still doubters who do not believe that what goes on in our heads profoundly affects the health of our bodies. Some people do not want to believe, because if the brain has such power over what happens in our bodies, then we might have to watch our attitudes if we wish to remain healthy. Others gladly accept such responsibility in return for the control bestowed on each of us in contributing to our own physical destinies. [27]

OUR PATTERNS OF RESPONSE

Early sensory experiences are programmed by how we are initially treated. When an experience is repeated, it becomes a pattern. How we interpret that experience is a "premature cognitive commitment"--premature," because it is made at an early stage of our development, "cognitive," because it programs our senses in a certain, fixed way, and "commitment," because it fixes us to a certain reality.

Our premature cognitive commitments imprison us in structure we call reality. Our sensory experience is structured in such a way that it shapes the very anatomy and physiology of our nervous system, so that ultimately the nervous system serves only one function --to reinforce what has now become a core belief system. It is the interpretation of our initial premature experiences that are the basis of how we live the remainder of our lives. It is these core belief systems that we must uncover and address. Then we can commit our lives to being aware of that to which we are committed, and to choose the consequences of that awareness.

Numerous illustrations of this phenomenon exist in our world today.

Fish, raised in one half of a tank divided by a piece of clear glass, will continue to use only that portion when the glass is removed. The glass that has been removed remains a sensory barrier although, in reality, it no longer exists.

House flies, raised in a jar with a top on it, will remain in the jar and not fly out when the top is removed.

Elephants, bound to a tree with a rope when they are young, can be held to a twig by a string as adults.

Autistic children can be taught to stand securely holding a rope tied between two chairs. With practice the children will stand up, hold on to the rope for support, and walk from one chair to the other. In time, a string can be substituted for the rope. Then the children can be given a string alone, not tied to anything, and they will walk unaided. If the string is taken away, the children will fall down. It is belief in the string that enables the child to walk. [28]

Our behavior is predictable because we become what we feel. What we think about expands into our reality. [29] We are the end product of our experiences and the interpretation of those experiences. Emotion is the energy our body carries about what we believe; symptoms and illness are one way our body communicates.

John Bradshaw states that our bodies carry the pain of our wounded inner child. He emphasizes that we can live our daily lives and not realize the sadness and rage is going on inside our bodies. We will act out our unresolved issues. Our belief systems ensure that we will act toward others, or ourselves, in a way that we were acted upon. Our neuronal gates can close down to the emotions, just as the fish become closed down to one side of the fish tank, just as flies refuse to escape to the outside world, the elephant fails to know his own strength and the autistic children miss thie ability to walk. We also become closed to our limitless potential. [30]

If we allow ourselves to remain in the prison of our original experiences, then we allow ourselves to be cramped into a space that, in reality, has no walls, no doors, no barriers, and no limits, except those of our own making.

The essence of psychological change is going beyond existing belief systems to the establishment of new principles in place of old patterns. The old belief systems are not always altered or eliminated. Instead, alternatives are added, so that our choice repertoire becomes enlarged, more flexible, and more complex.

In order to alter, eliminate, or enhance our repertoire of choices within existing belief systems, it is essential to know what they are. The pattern of our behavior, on every level and in every instance, depends on our interactions with our initial care-givers throughout our developmental stages. These interactions established the laws that unequivocally govern all of our subsequent perceptions, feelings, and behaviors. These initial interactions with our primary care-givers form the essential building blocks for our personality development.

CHANGING OUR BELIEF SYSTEMS

I can contribute personal testimony to how a belief system can be changed. My mother was raised never to "toot her own horn," and she felt that I should be raised that way also. As a result, she did not "toot my horn" either. [31] I heard her tell friends or relatives who had never seen me or had not seen me for awhile, "Alice is not very pretty, but she has a great personality." One aunt looked through the window of the car where I was sitting and said to my mother, "She's not that ugly." I translated my mother's consistent behavior into the *belief system* that I was indeed ugly.

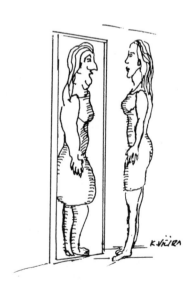

What you see may not be what you are.

When people befriended me, I believed that they were being nice because they felt sorry for me. I would do everything in my power to make them comfortable, thus perpetuating the belief that "she has a good personality." I never looked in the mirror except cursorily, and then at specific areas, not my entire face. I remember reading *Elephant Man* 32 and feeling that I knew exactly how he must have felt.

This *belief system* existed until I was 27 years old and enrolled in a UCLA Sensitivity Training Seminar. The seminar consisted of a three-day weekend, a five-hour meeting each month for five months, and then an ending three-day session. The group consisted of fifteen members, twelve men and two women besides myself. During the third five-hour meeting, in the midst of a discussion of how I responded to a man whom seemed attracted to me the first weekend, Lou, the leader, said, "Alice, you don't feel at all attractive, do you?"

In that fraction of a second, I saw in the shocked expressions of the group members that this could possibly not be so. My first thought was, "They're surprised--they couldn't have faked that expression." My mother was wrong. I was not ugly. The primary insight was that I could look at myself and decide if I was "ugly" or not. I could make my own judgment about the way that I looked. There was a difference of opinion.

The important issue was that I *noticed*, and I *believed* them. I realized that I had some options. Change comes from a new *awareness* that we notice and believe.

When my old belief system changed, my life changed. I took a course at John Robert Powers to learn how to wear makeup, dress, accessorize my outfits--all skills I had not learned before because I felt it was useless. The most important change was that I heard compliments for the first time in my life. I cannot remember any compliment about my personal appearance until that meeting, and since that meeting I hear them all the time. Getting compliments was not something new. I had just screened them out because they had been in conflict with an existing belief system. They were incongruent with what I had come to believe.

What is not congruent with an existing belief system will be eliminated from *awareness*. A new belief system, a new cognitive map, is needed to bring in new information that is meaningful enough to alter or eliminate the previous beliefs. This is not an easy task to accomplish. But as Mark Twain said, "It is an amazing thing when we look at our attitudes and begin to perceive the world differently: others change."

I was able to change the belief system about my appearance because I learned to trust the people in my group and to believe their reactions. We had spent over forty therapeutic hours together, and the timing of Lou's question was perfect.

The magic, however, was not the question, but the shocked looks on the faces of the group members. Their reaction triggered an instantaneous "Ah Ha!" that changed my life, because it changed my belief system. I was able to look into the mirror and see myself for the first time through the eyes of these people, and no longer through the eyes of my mother.

When Lou said, "You do not feel at all attractive, do you?" he verbalized something that had never been spoken to me. He understood me in a deep way, and by a correct and well-timed intervention made me feel safe. He became, for a minute, the strong, protective parent who mirrored the belief system that had caused my pain. I felt treasured. The members of the group alleviated my lifelong feelings of loneliness. My belief system changed.

Changing beliefs takes work because we fight against feelings that deep down seem absolutely true to us. We were hypnotized into our beliefs and made premature commitments before we had a real choice.

OUR PROTECTIVE ARMOR

Figure 2 shows graphically how I see core belief systems housed in protective armor. *Belief systems* are formed as premature cognitive commitments are made, and behaviors consistent with that belief system are repeated. These behaviors are reactive because they were first used in response to a trauma. The response and the belief system reduce feelings of discomfort, so this behavior became reinforcing. In turn, our ego defense mechanisms protected that behavior in order to ensure survival and prevent any discomfort.

We must become aware of the elaborate system of habitual feelings, thoughts, and automatic behaviors we have accumulated. This system molds us into the special people we are, but at the same time, it is the source of all our troubles.

Figure 2
Belief Systems in Protective Armor

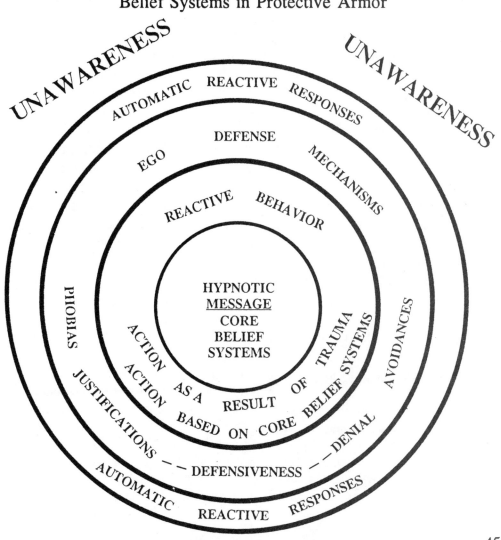

45

Once we take a defensive stance, we revert into automatic reactive behaviors. We become the person whose behavior is ruled by a premature cognitive commitment. When we defend a position, we further our commitment to that position. That defense strengthens the protective armor.

If we defend being a victim, we remain a victim. If we have defended taking care of others at our own expense, then we remain co-dependent. If we never felt loveable or loved, and defend our automatic actions that reinforce that feeling, then we continue to feel unlovable. If we felt powerless in our relationship with our parents, and defend them, then we may develop a passive-aggressive personality to maintain our own inner sense of power.

Our behavior becomes automatic. Our feelings are tucked away beyond our awareness. When we go against or challenge these core issues, we grow too uncomfortable, so we revert to automatic responses that are familiar. Many of our premature cognitive commitments were pre-verbal, internalized before we had words to deal with them. These automatic behaviors cannot be changed unless the underlying belief system can be identified and examined.

We can discover what our belief systems are only by asking ourselves why we operate the way we do, and being willing to open ourselves up to what basic beliefs exist. We need to understand what belief systems were formed when crucial developmental tasks were not successfully negotiated. (See Table 1) We need to recognize the difference between how we defend against a reality of the past, and the reality that is *now*.

A client of mine, attempting to illustrate for me why he was so stuck in therapy, drew me this picture (figure 3) and described it in the following way:

> I will do anything to avoid the pain. I will do almost anything to avoid anger. I have been willing to survive as much as possible in 'rational' (superficial) everyday living. It has not provided joy, but it has kept me at arm's length from pain. It has also kept me at arm's length from *me*. The core of *me* is tied to pain, and I have been unwilling to confront the pain in order to find *me*. Freedom from pain has been of greater value than self-knowledge and self-love. If I can blame God, then I am not responsible for my situation. If I can blame my wife, my parents, Alice,

group, life, etc., then I am not responsible. (Of course, if I am not responsible, then I cannot *change* anything, either.) I can just remain stuck, blaming everyone, and enjoying the luxury of inaction.

Figure 3
Avoidance of Me

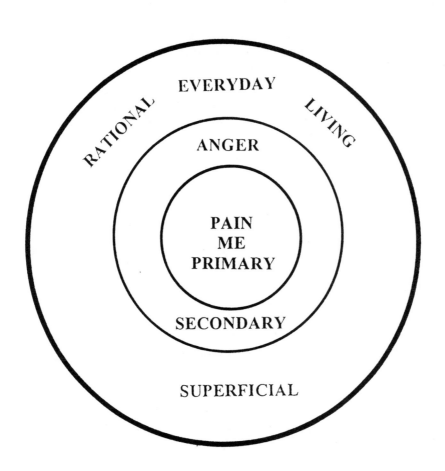

My client's wisdom in describing how he continues to protect himself will enable him to look into his belief systems in order to begin to expressing the anger, and find himself.

> Rob separated from his wife because he did not feel he was a priority in her life and he was unhappy. Jackie did not want a divorce and wanted to work on the relationship. When they got together, instead of telling her his feelings, he would initiate sex--a familiar, comfortable activity. In doing this, he avoided the anger and the pain of feeling unimportant to her. Having sex with Jackie did not make Rob feel any closer to her and their relationship was at a standstill. Until he was willing to experience the anxiety and discomfort of talking about his feelings, the separation and marriage remained unchanged.

The next two chapters describe personality, identitiy, roles we play, self-esteem we have for each of these parts, and ego in relation to our *self-in-process*.

CHAPTER 5

PERSONALITY, IDENTITY, AND ROLES WE PLAY WITHIN OUR SELF-IN-PROCESS

"I've learned that if I persevere
in the right direction I will prevail.
The obstacles I overcome are learning experiences and
not failures but corrections on my course."
—Larry Moore

I prefer to call the self the *self-in-process*, which describes the active, dynamic nature of the self. From birth, the *self-in-process* on takes on an ego, ego functions, an actual body, a body image, an "identity," a "personality," a conscience (personal and social), a spiritual essence that some call a soul, a super-ego, a "higher self" or part of what is called the universal consciousness, and all the hyphenated "selves," including self-concept, self-esteem, self-worth, self-image, and so forth. The *self-in-process* is the total, essential, all-encompassing being of an individual.

A SELF-IN-PROCESS

Claudia is a real estate broker making upward of $200,000/year. She is well-liked, with several very good friends. She is close to her family, often spending time with her brother's children, and happily and actively participates in all family functions. She is health-conscious, fit and impeccably groomed. She has a great personality. But she was caught up in her roles as daughter, sister, aunt, girlfriend, friend, and "doer." She identified only with the roles she played, and she was unhappy. As long as she kept up with her roles and upbeat personality, she had positive self-esteem and a positive self-concept.

Claudia came to me very depressed, suffering from anxiety attacks and severe, debilitating headaches. She was an adult child of an alcoholic and had been molested by her father. No one in the family ever mentioned either the alcoholism or the molestation. Claudia had no idea who she was outside of the roles she played and the activities she participated in. She was in a long term relationship with an alcoholic who mistreated her. Claudia survived only in these roles, and her self was not allowed to emerge. She functioned perfectly for everyone else, but not all for herself.

As we worked together, Claudia began to examine her core belief system that she needed to be "a good girl and not cause any trouble." She broke up with her boyfriend and began to evaluate the friends who used and took advantage of her. She began to consider the requests her family members made of her, rather than always saying "yes" regardless of her own plans or priorities. Her headaches began to subside. The anxiety attacks stopped and her depression lifted. Her self was beginning to emerge and be in-process.

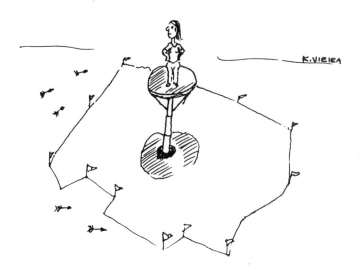

**As soon as Claudia set clear boundaries,
the anxiety attacks stopped and she was
lifted out of the depression**

The commonly-known parts of the self-in-process, other than the ego, are our identities and the roles we play, our personality, and the feelings we have about these parts of our self-in-process.

Figure 4
Components of the Self-In-Process

IDENTITIES ARE FLEETING

Our identity is the role or roles we play consistently over time and that "work." The role or roles we learn to play are acceptable in that we feel safe within a role. We are different in each of our roles. We may have a role as a child, a student, a mother, a father, a psychologist, a photographer, a student and so on.

Our identity is fleeting in that we change it if it doesn't "work." We can be said to "assume an identity" that possesses certain qualities that may or may not be consistent with the authenticity of our feelings. This identity may be in service of our ego, or in service of our self-in-process. Our sense of identity usually arises out of belonging to a specified group, not of being someone. Each role or identity has a different self-esteem and self-image.

When I'm functioning as a psychologist, my self-esteem and the image I have of myself is very positive. When I'm functioning as a photographer, my self-esteem and image of myself is less positive, because I am still an amateur photographer.

> Laura sells illegal drugs. The identity she projects to the people who buy from her is completely different from the identity she employs with her family and the PTA (from which her illicit occupation is a secret).

If we define our self-in-process by the roles we play, then we are "selling ourselves short," and not in touch with the essence of our beings. We are much, much more than the roles we play!

CIRCUS ATTIRE   CITY CIRCUS ATTIRE

We carry a feeling within our self-in-process about each identity. The way we identify ourselves changes. We might have identified with the "flower children" in the sixties and now have a positive or negative sense of our self as a result of that identity. We may have had a positive self-concept then, but a negative self-concept now--about that same identity. We do not usually define our self-in-process by the roles we play.

When I felt that "having a good personality" was required of me, I was able to act as an interesting person. It was the role I played. But that person was not really me. It was the me that I had heard my mother describe when she talked to her friends. This good-personality role was in service of my defenses (and my mother). It was not in service of my self-in-process.

A "good guy" personality, is a mask we put on to project a good image when we feel that we are not "good." A "tough guy" personality role is a mask we wear when we feel scared inside.

A "tough guy" says things such as "I don't need them," they're a bunch of losers anyway," "I only need myself," and "I can handle it," when deep inside his ego is screaming to be loved in reaction to the unworthiness that the "tough guy" feels.

> Warren is a 35-year-old man, large in stature and a construction worker by trade. He entered into group therapy because he was unable to relate to his wife, family, and friends. He spent most of his time alone. When "bugged by his wife" to spend time with her, he would throw a tantrum by yelling and calling her a "nag"--saying she was never satisfied. The truth of the matter was that he did not know how to relate in an interpersonal, empathetic manner. His family consisted of isolated individuals who did not speak to one another unless there was a disagreement. Warren never learned to relate positively. His defense was being a "tough guy" who claimed he didn't need anyone or want anyone in his life. His wife divorced him, and he says of her, "I had to get rid of the bitch."

Bob faced another day ahead of riding his ill-mannered, wild horse Josie. Time to wear his "tough guy" mask.

The more subtle "*tough guy*" is the person who needs to have his view accepted but does not care what means he uses to get his/her way.

Ross blocks everyone's ideas by claiming that "the others' ideas are *ridiculous*." Ross is bored by, and often interrupts conversations that are not of his choosing. When Ross is not the focus of attention and he cannot turn the focus toward himself, he is silent and pouts. He tells himself that the others in his group are *too stupid to understand* the help *he* is able to give them.

55

OUR PERSONALITY IS RELATIVELY PERMANENT

Our personality is the way we relate socially. Our personality is more than the role or identity that we assume. It is a bit confusing because of the interchange of terns when the phrase "good personality", "tough-guy personality" and so on are used. Among psychiatrists the term "personality" is used almost in its original sense like the masks worn on the stage by actors in ancient Rome. The personality is like a mask in the sense that it consists of patterns of behavior through which the individual expresses his inner interests. [33]

Henry Murray, one of the leading psychologists of our time, defines personality as "an abstract structure of the mind., with a series of events spanning the entire lifetime, reflecting enduring and recurring elements of behavior." [34]

ENDURING DISPOSITIONS

When we change, we do so within the context of our personality or (according to Jung) enduring "dispositions" with which we were born. Jung's definition of persona is the definition of personality that describes best the personality within the self: "a mask which is worn by a person in response to the demands of social convention and tradition and to his own inner disposition." [35]

Jung said that we are born either extraverted or introverted, sensing or intuitive, feeling or thinking, judging or perceiving. The composition of how these traits are put together results in a personality type. Isabel Myers, a researcher in applications of personality type, and her mother, Katheryn Briggs, developed a test to facilitate our awareness about the general personality types Jung described. She called the test the Myers/Briggs Personality Type Indicator for the Constructive Use of Differences. Myers describes four basic personality types and a total of sixteen variations on the four basic types. [36]

56

The four basic types are:

The Catalyst makes things to happen, whose priority is humanity, and who values integrity, authenticity, meaning and worth;

The Visionary has great ideas (usually for others to follow-through on) whose priorities are knowledge, competency, and ability;

The Traditionalist is the detail and follow-through person whose priorities are duty, social solidarity and maintaining the status-quo;

The Trouble-Shooter is the negotiator whose priorities are joy, freedom, spontaneity, action and independence. [37]

Jung believed that Trouble-Shooter would always be Trouble-Shooter. A Catalyst would always a Catalyst and so on. He believed that change within that disposition is possible, but changing from that disposition is not.

> I am a Catalyst, and my husband is a Visionary. If I know that his ideas are going to be wonderful and that he is approaches possibilities with impersonal analysis. He knows that my focus is what is happening now with people is my focus and that I approach the now with personal analysis. Because I am more emotional, we make a perfect team.
>
> If I, however, get upset at him for not considering my feelings when he is "creating," then I do him a dis-service because I am not honoring his unique personality. By the same token, if he becomes irritated with me for pushing for feelings and task completion, then he is not honoring my unique personality. Only if we accept each other's unique personalities can we increase the awareness and the full potential of our *selves-in-process*.

SELF-CONCEPT, SELF-ESTEEM, AND SELF-IMAGE

Personality development is not wholly dependent on experiences in the first five years of life. The struggle to be whole, to "fit into society and feel a part" goes on for our entire lives. This is why awareness is vitally important in our continued efforts to develop our self-in-process.

Self-concept, self-esteem and self-image can only be understood in terms of existing belief systems.

A positive *self-concept* can exist only if our self-image is congruent with how others see us. There needs to be a "fit" between who we want to be or feel we are, and how others see us. A man who believes himself to be noble and giving, but whom others see as selfish and afraid, will feel the incongruence. This incongruence will cause him pain and result in a poor *self-concept*. We may need a *"tough guy"* self-image to cover up a poor *self-concept*. I needed a "good personality" self-image to cover up feeling unacceptable in other ways. I appeared to be a "happy girl" but inside I had a negative self-concept.

Self-esteem is a feeling that we have about ourselves when we experience a series of successes that are based in reality--that is, based on a congruence between what we feel inside and what we feel from the outside. *Self-esteem* is based on having a realistic view of our strengths and weaknesses. It is a realistic confidence we have about our self-in-process. If our belief systems are based on reality within an individuated self-in-process, our self-esteem and *self-concept* will be positive. If our belief systems are limiting and self-defeating, our *self-esteem* and our *self-concept* will be negative.

Our *self-image* is the way we address ourselves. We act the way we feel we are. When our self-image is very low, we sometimes erect cover-ups to maintain or protect our self-concept.

There are a number of behaviors that protect a poor *self-image:*

Self-Image Protection Behavior

DEFENSIVE BEHAVIOR	BELIEFS ABOUT SELF
The Blamer projects out his own feelings of unworthiness by fault-finding, controlling techniques of criticism, name-calling and anger.	"I am frightened so I use verbal messages to make you frightened. I feel like a nothing, so I must treat you like I am a something so you will obey me."
The Blocker acts out by preventing others from doing anything at all; he is a "wet blanket," "raining on everyone's parade."	"I can be important if I stop them from making a mistake."
The Conformist agrees with everyone and never disagrees. No one knows what the conformist really thinks.	"I can make everyone happy by pleasing them and making critical people feel that I totally support them. Then they will like me."
The Disrupter acts out by using irrelevant statements, jokes and disclaimers. He changes the subject, is hyperactive and tries to take attention away from his problem.	"I'm unlovable and can't stand to see people get upset so I'll act up. Pay attention to me and my inappropriate behavior and you will forget the conflict."

The Intellectual rationalizes and uses logic in an above-it-all behavior, withdrawing and distancing from problems, not disclosing directly.

"I'll act super-intelligent, bored and above it all, so I won't have to face the problem."

The Pleaser (co-dependent) agrees with everything in order to keep the other person happy. The Pleaser apologizes for anything and is a "yes" person.

"I'm nothing. You are every-everything." [38]

THE INTERPLAY BETWEEN EGO AND SELF
AS IT RELATES TO CHANGE

"A human being, thus, is at all times
an organism, an ego, and a member of a society."
—Erik Erikson

"I discriminate between the Ego and the Self,
since the Ego is only the subject of my consciousness,
while the Self is the subject of my whole totality.
In this sense, the Self would be an ideal factor
which embraces and includes the Ego."
—Carl Jung

"Wherever ego I go"
—David Zasloff

"You just don't get it!"

"He appears rigid and stuck."

Group therapy members hammer into Rick
as he desperately resorts to his posture
of defensive foxhole digging.

Rick was rigid, stuck in his views. When anyone challenged what he wanted to do, his defenses kicked in and he would immediately give away his power by reacting. A fellow group member told Rick, "You just don't get it." Rick became irate, defensive and infuriated. I suggested that instead of reacting, he had the option of checking out the congruence of his experience with the other group members. He asked, and each member of the group agreed that he appeared out of touch and rigid in his way of thinking. Rick was surprised, but he was interested in how he came across to others. He said, "Inside my body, I felt I did 'get it,' that I and was flexible and open, but I now can see that I'm not."

DEFINING EGO VERSUS SELF

Rick's first reaction is an ego reaction, and his second response is that of a person coming into his *self-in-process.*

The terms *self* and *ego* are often used interchangeably, but they should not be. Lumping them together eliminates the possibility of distinguishing the self-in-process from the ego. The ego is only part of the self-in-process, similar to the way our identities are part of our personality. The ego's influence on the self-in-process, and how it functions to help or hinder the self-in-process, is the subject of this chapter.

Heintz Kohut defines the ego as the experiences that happened to us long ago (the "there and then" experiences). The ego is completely subjective. The "self" is the sum total of what is happening now (the "here and now" experience). Our self-in-process sees the whole and reacts to situations in context, rather than in terms of the past or in terms of being safe. The self-in-process is more objective. [39]

The ego learns to cope with our environment and the people in it, whereas the self-in-process understands ourselves and our relationship to others. Who we are when our ego remains fragile and dependent, is attached to "there and then" events. When we are able to be introspective and not defend our "there and then" position, our emerging self-in-process is no longer dependent, and can be focused on the "here and now" events.

John Bradshaw makes a similar distinction between what he calls the essential self, or "wonder child" (which I refer to as the self-in-process), and the adapted self or wounded self (what I call the ego). Bradshaw emphasizes that the ego is always unauthentic when it is compared to the self-in-process. The self-in-process is the child, who exists as a loved and valued human being and feels essential to mother. The ego is the limited sphere of consciousness, used to adjust to the demands of family and culture. The ego is limited by survival needs. It is the part of the self-in-process that is rooted in our family and the culture into which we were born.

Bradshaw makes a critical point about the potential for changing limiting belief systems. He states that all cultural and family systems are relative, because they represent only one of many possible ways to understand and interpret reality. As children, we see our family and cultural mores as the only possible choices. Even if our ego adaptation were fully functioning in relation to our family and culture, it would still be limited and fragmented in relation to our true selves. [40]

This is not to deny that the ego has a purpose. The ego must be integrated and functional if we are to survive and cope with daily life. In fact, a strong integrated ego gives us a sense of confidence, control, and responsibility for the development of our self-in-process. Once integrated, the ego becomes our source of strength. Our self-in-process motivates us to look at our child of the "there and then" experiences so that we can work through the issues and people that participated in our less-than-full development.

In everyday language, we hear people refer to others as having a *big ego,* or a *fragile ego.*

> Charles Barkley, a professional basketball player for the Phoenix Suns was named the National Basketball Association's Most Valuable Player in 1993. He was sometimes booed when he came on the court because of his arrogance. Barkley was said to have a *big* ego.
>
> Conversely, a tennis player who is completely thrown off his game when someone questions his line calls, is said to have a "weak" or *fragile* ego.

64

FRAGILE EGO

"All I said to him was, 'Are you sure
the ball was out?' And he just fell apart!"

RESOLVING PAST ISSUES

When our ego is strong enough to be incorporated into, rather than hinder, our self-in-process, the "there and then" can be resolved so that the "here and now" can take precedence. The most important "there and then" experiences are issues that we have not resolved with our parents. These issues are "the most important," because if we don't recognize and resolve them, we will repeat them unconsciously. Recognizing and becoming aware of unhealthy patterns in our lives is essential.

Don was brutally beaten by his mother when he was a child. His two older sisters would blame him for all their wrong-doings and his mother would believe her daughters and beat Don. On one occasion, he ran from her when she was hitting him with a fire iron, she threw it and it lodged in his side. Don is now 80 years old, and continues to be victimized by people stealing from him, lying about him and being blamed for situations for which he clearly had no part. He has erected his life in such a way to be the "scapegoat." When discussing his mother, he refers to her "as a saint." "She always loved me and would do anything for me." Don's issues wtih his mother remain unresloved.

By repeating unresolved issues that are tied to our early belief systems, the surviving ego keeps us from focusing on a broader, more pervasive concern about who we really are. We remain attached to obtaining something that we did not receive the first time we needed it. That means we will attract people with problems similar to people who have hurt us in our families. We will attempt unsuccessfully to do in the present, what needed to be done in the past. Resolving the issues of the "there and then" experience is essential in order to fully experience the "here and now."

Each of the functions of the ego can serve our total health, or its functions can remain in the survival mode and prohibit our growth. Rational thinking is usually thought of as a positive ego function, used in problem-solving and adaptation. But it can also become invested with defensive meanings.

A young girl may rationally conclude that to marry early is the only way to flee from the sexual, physical, or emotional abuse of her parents. Her ability to flee is an adaptive response, rational in its origins, but leaving home before her development needs are met, may impair the girl's ability to accept adult responsibility, sexual intimacy, and child-rearing.

Donna is a 25-year-old, divorced woman with two children, ages 10 and 6. She had been repeatedly raped by her brother. Her mother, who was aware of, but did not stop the sexual abuse, called Donna a "dirty child." Donna was mother to her younger siblings whenever her mother had other plans, and that responsibility gravely interfered with Donna's schooling. Donna became pregnant with her first child at 15 and

66

subsequently married the 16-year-old boy who had fathered the child. She felt that getting married was the only way to flee the family situation.

When her daughter, Annie, began growing up, Donna began to resent her because Annie received the attention and experiences Donna had not been given.

Developmentally, Donna was impaired in her ability to accept responsibility for her family, her sexual intimacy with her husband, and child-rearing. She began leaving the house when her husband came home from work and not returning until morning. She refused to have sex with her husband after the conception of their second child, and she competed with her children, treating them as rivals instead of nurturing them.

Another example of letting ego functions serve the ego instead of the *self-in-process* can be observed in this account of John, who appears to have it all together in every way.

John, age 40, is a stockbroker. He lives and breathes Wall Street. He invests for his clients, his parents and himself. He talks "stocks" and entertains his friends with tales about the business community and economics of the world, based on the stock market. John works 15 to 18 hours every day, seven days a week. He is financially very successful. He also has severe panic attacks when he is not working.

John is obviously a successful business person--outgoing, aggressive, financially secure, fearless, and seemingly free from major difficulties. But he is a workaholic who, without work, cannot function adequately. Work is the organizer of his personality. Hard work and productivity are attributes of a healthy self-in-process, but used to this extent, they serve as a defense against dealing with the interpersonal issues that John faces.

In the next chapter we look at what can go wrong with our ego and the self-in-process.

WHAT DETERMINES THE HEALTH OF OUR SELF-IN-PROCESS?

"Each of us must go back into our past, back into our early family life, and see how this habit was formed. Seeing its inception keeps our way of controlling in consciousness. Remember, most of our family members were operating in a drama themselves, trying to pull energy out of us as children. This is why we had to form a control drama in the first place. We had to have a strategy to win energy back. It is always in relations to our family members that we develop our particular dramas. However, once we recognize the energy dynamics in our families, we can go past these control strategies and see what was really happening."...

"You said you help them find their true self, how?"

"There is only one way. Each of us has to go back to our family experience, that childhood time and place, and review what happened. Once we become conscious of our control drama, then we can focus on the higher truth of our family, the silver lining so to speak, that lies beyond the energy conflict. Once we find this truth, it can energize our lives, for this truth tells us who we are, the path we are on, what we are doing."

—James Redfield

Four characteristics must be present in mother if we are to grow up healthy. They are empathy, mirroring, average expectable environment, and good-enough mothering.

EMPATHY

Empathy is an intellectual understanding of what is inherently foreign to us. To empathize is to recognize and identify another person's feelings, emotions, and sufferings through observation. It is not necessary to have experienced those feelings to know and understand, intellectually, what the other person needs. To empathize is to place ourself in another's position, and to identify closely with another's circumstance.

Heintz Kohut developed the Psychology of the Self, a new dimension in psychology, in the late 1970s. In a talk he gave two days before his death, he corrected the false impression that empathy was merely a way of showing sympathy and gentle understanding. He used the example of Nazi empathy in relation to Londoners during World War II.

The Nazis put a screaming device on the bombs they dropped on England, because they knew that the sound would terrify the British. With this screaming device, bombs from far away could be heard, and the effect of the bombing was magnified. The Nazis' empathy was a method of activating the understanding of another's experience--not of caring or having compassion. [40]

We need mother to have soothing empathy--knowing what we need and soothingly respond to our needs, almost before we have them. Mother needs to *know* that we are wet before we cry about it.

MIRRORING

Mirroring differs from empathy in that empathy can be felt for a person or about a situation without any actual overt behavior. Mirroring an action is having another person stamp it with approval or recognition after we act in a certain way or have a feeling that is recognized and validated. The Nazis did not mirror the Londoners, quite the contrary, the Nazis' empathy enabled them to manipulate the Londoners.

Mirroring, in the best sense of the word, is *active (verbal and non-verbal) listening*. When we are infants, we need to be noticed. Our actions and feelings need to be reflected. Every action, word, gesture, expression, or tone of voice on the part of our parents conveyed a message about our value and worth. Mirroring provides us with a frame of reference. As our actions are reflected in the eyes of our mother (primarily), we develop a frame of reference from which we see ourselves.

When we are not adequately mirrored we fill that void with belief systems that make some sense of not feeling good about ourselves. We adjust reality as I did when I heard my mother say I was not pretty.

> Beth, a two-year-old, was sorting through her toys. When she could not find the toy she was looking for, she began to scream. Her mother adequately mirrored her by telling her "Beth, you feel very angry because your doll is not in the box. It is very frustrating that you cannot find what you want when you want it."

An unhealthy, unmirrored, response by Beth's mother would have been to tell Beth, "If you keep screaming, you'll have to go to your room."

An example of the difference between mirroring and empathy:

> Jane's husband came in from work right before the couple was to go out, looking exhausted. Empathetically, Jane can see and feel how tired he is. She can mirror his situation by saying, "Wow, you look like you would prefer to stay home tonight instead of going to the Smiths."

AVERAGE EXPECTABLE ENVIRONMENT

An *average expectable environment* is one in which we learn to feel from the very beginning that our presence is acceptable. We learn that having needs, like needing to be fed, touched and taken care of, is part of being. We learn that we can be just as we are without the anxiety of having to fit our needs into someone else's schedule.

Many studies about the feeding of infants and animals show that if they are held, cuddled, and "cooed" at while being fed are healthier than those who are merely fed for sustenance.

A study conducted on rabbits to test levels of cholesterol showed the rabbits that were fed greater and greater amounts of cholesterol died. But in one cage of rabbits lived much longer, and it was discovered that the man who fed the rabbits in this cage loved animals. Instead of throwing the food into the cage, he held the rabbits as he fed them.

Probably the most famous study on this subject was done by Renee Spitz during World War II on hundreds of babies in an orphanage in France. All the babies were fed, but only half of them were held and fed. A great percentage of the babies that were not held died. [41]

At first, we are one with our mothers. We are totally dependent. We become aware of pain from the shock of birth, and later from being hungry, cold, and wet. Pleasure comes from being fed, being dried, and being warmed. If we cry because we are hungry, and we are picked up and fed in a consistent manner, we learn that our pain will be relieved. We also learn that someone cares about this pain and will relieve it. This is considered an average expectable environment. [42]

If, on the other hand, we cry because we are hungry and no one feeds us, and this happens consistently, we will fear the pain because the pain is not predictably relieved by our caretaker. Then we must learn to handle the pain by ourselves. The way we do this is to seal off the pain and not feel it. We dissociate ourselves from an average expectation of pain relief. Without the connection that relieves pain, we learn to feel very early that we are not important. This is not considered an average expectable environment.

GOOD-ENOUGH MOTHERING

Good-enough mothering is a term coined by D. W. Winnicott. Good-enough mothering is similar to the average expectable environment but it is more specific. Good-enough mothering requires that our mother be preoccupied with our needs so that we have a *continuity of our being.* We need to be shielded from all impingements so that we can evolve and create our own external world (the first separation.) The good-enough mother *holds* us and relieves us from any possible anxiety. The good-enough mother holding us gives us our first set of boundaries and becomes the organizer of our first experiences. Her preoccupation with our needs makes her good-enough. The average expectable environment presupposes frustration and makes the first separation possible, but initially a good-enough mother is essential to our developing self-in-process. Her preoccupation with our needs is essential so we do not feel interfered with by the outside world. [43]

THE DEVELOPMENT OF SELF-IN-PROCESS

The first juncture in the development of self-in-process is the realization that we are not the same as our mothers. This usually occurs between six to nine months. The second juncture begins when we are assured that we can explore the world with our mother's approval, between 18 months and three years. The third juncture takes place when we learn we are on our own and we leave home, between 18 and 21 years. At each juncture successful separation enables our self-in-process to lift our experiences to a higher level of organization and strengthen our confidence in our own subjective reality, which may be different from that of our mother's. [44]

This section discusses the first two of these junctures because of their crucial impact on the development of belief systems, the role our self-in-process will play in our lives as growing individuals, and the role our ego will play in helping us survive. The third juncture is discussed in Chapter 18.

VALIDATION POINTS

Three successful validation points are necessary in order to be a self-in-process, to have positive outcomes in the stages of development. (See Table 1)

From womb to 6-9 months

1st Validation/Separation	OR	1st Injury: Unhealthy Attachment
Baby sees self as same as mother in positive attachment with: soothing empathy good-enough mothering average expectable environment mirroring		Baby is inadequately attached because of lack of empathy, a mother pre-occupied with something other than baby
assuring trust		resulting in mistrust
baby can separate and has the first sense of self		*baby remains unhealthily attached and has a distorted sense of self*

From 6-9 months to 3 years:

2nd Validation/Separation	OR	2nd Injury: Unhealthy Attachment
Autonomy is established to enhance the first sense of self		Shame and doubt take the place of autonomy. Ego functions take on a defensive nature geared to survival
assuring autonomy child can do things without mother in constant watchfulness the child develops an		resulting in child doing little without feeling guilty and bad about self
enhanced sense of self		*damaged sense of self*

From 3 years to 18+ years

3rd Validation/Separation	OR	Lifetime of Co-Dependency and Passive-Aggressiveness
Out of autonomy grows		Without autonomy, child develops

initiative	inferiority
industry	lack of clear identity
identity	isolation
assuring	resulting in
individuation	*no individuation*
further enhancement	continued attachment
of self-in-process	and dependency on
	approval and
	acknowledgment from
	family of origin or
	replicas thereof

During our first few months of life, we experience our mother as a part of ourselves. There is no boundary between us. We begin our lives feeling totally self-centered in that we feel the world revolves completely around us. Michael Balient describes our physiological state by using a comparison: we are as dependent on our relationship to our emotional environment as we are on our relationship to air.

> We cannot live without it; we inhale it order to take parts out of it and use them as we want; then after putting substances into it that we want to get rid of, we exhale it - without paying the slightest attention to it. In fact, the air must be there for us, and as long as it is there in sufficient supply and quality, we do not take any notice of it...we do not consider it separate from us; we just use it. The situation changes abruptly if the environment is altered....It is an idle question to enquire whether air in our lungs, or in our bowels, is us or not us, or where the exact boundary between us and the air is. [44]

THE FIRST SEPARATION

In the first of the three major stages of *separation* from total dependency, we realize for the first time that we are not the same as our mother, and the first validation of the self-in-process takes place.

It is difficult to determine the exact age when we acquire the sense of self that comes from feeling safely separate from mother. This concept of feeling safely separate is crucial in our development.

Until we are nine months old, we do not differentiate ourselves from our mothers. In the very early months, "I" is not different from the "Not-I." This is especially true if loving and consistent care is given as our needs arise. The realization that "I" is indeed different from "not I" is an unpleasant reality.

Regardless of how perfect mother tries to be, there will be times when we will meet with an unempathetic or disappointing response from her. The quality, the timing, and the quantity of these inevitable failures determine the premature cognitive commitments, and thus our core belief systems.

THE NEED FOR EMPATHY IN DEVELOPMENT
OF SELF-IN-PROCESS

Assuming an average expectable environment, a good-enough mother will empathize with us completely. Her soothing empathy is as much a part of the average expectable environment as is temperature control, shelter, satiation of hunger, nurturance, holding, and touching. The importance of this soothing empathy in developing our sense of self cannot be minimized. It is as important as the air we breathe.

If, however, our mother is not good-enough, there is no continuity of our being, and therefore we cannot feel a sense of self. Without this sense, we feel as stifled and desperate as we would without enough air. In essence, our mother's soothing, empathetic preoccupation with us enables us to live and develop in spite of our inability to control any part of our environment. At first, this need for protection is absolute. We have no awareness of our mother, just as we have no awareness of breathing air--unless we do not have it. The first awareness of mother is when she is not there. These periods of mother not being there must be minimal, like holding our breath or being denied air. We can be without breath momentarily, but we cannot be deprived of air or mother for too long!

THE SECOND SEPARATION

In the second phase of development, beginning at about nine months, activity becomes the most important task. We separate in short bursts from our mother. 46 The most important function for mother in this stage is to serve as the mirroring frame of reference for us. This means that we act independently for a brief moment, and then we look quickly at mother to *see how we did*. Mother serves as a mirror for us to see ourselves. We reach out and explore with our eyes and arms, and mother responds. Her selective response, acknowledging our accomplishment, gradually alters our behavior. What emerges is our unique personality and individuality.

When mother is not comfortable with her mothering skills, or she is distracted for some other reason, she may not pay appropriate attention. Then our "mirror" is either absent or distorted. The quality of the caretaking tasks (rather than the tasks themselves) will affect us for the rest of our lives.

Any breakdown of these first two crucial separations leads to a lifetime of inner conflict and vulnerability (see Table 1). A traumatic breakdown of this sort results in our inability to know our own feelings. If we do not know how we feel, we cannot act on our feelings, and we are unable to take care of ourselves. These early relationship dynamics form the foundation of the belief systems that cause us immeasurable trouble as we negotiate the remainder of our lives.

"Mommy, when you are done with mirror,
I am sad, I am hungry and cold."

"Timmy, I think it will partly
cloudy today with showers forecasted.
I'm going to wear my spring flower dress."

THE NEED FOR MIRRORING
IN DEVELOPMENT OF SELF-IN-PROCESS

Our mother's preoccupation with us and her soothing empathy in the average expectable environment cannot provide for perfection in all things. Through the very act of living, we begin to experience degrees of frustration, deprivation, and restraint. These unpleasant feelings must be real enough for us to overcome the feeling of being one with mother, but they cannot be severe enough that we feel abandoned and helpless. This balance is achieved when our good-enough mother mirrors our feelings about the delays. Normal delays and momentary frustrations set the stage for the time that our mother gradually relaxes her preoccupation with us. If mother is unpredictable, unstable, anxious, or depressed, then we are deprived of a reliable frame of reference. Our beliefs about the world will differ from what they would be with her appropriate regard. With a reliable frame of reference or mirror, we can focus on our own progress and feel equal to any challenge.

EGO'S ROLE IN BLOCKING AWARENESS

Ego development is different from the development of the *self-in-process*. The ego is that part of our makeup that mediates between our *self* and everything else. Its prime function is to figure out what we need to do in response to demands made on us. Early demands about what is "right" or what we "should do" are placed on us by society. These societal values include traditions, religious or ethnic teachings, and moral directives. In addition, we have to respond to our parental and familial demands and expectations, as well as to our own internal needs, emotional states, and fantasies.

To meet these overwhelming and often contradictory demands, the ego develops many functions, one of which is ego defense mechanisms. Ego defense mechanisms are formed for our survival. When we feel threatened or unloved in any way, the ego defense mechanisms serve to reduce conflict and anxiety, and this one function of the ego keeps us from the self-in-process and from exploring our core belief systems. The ego has an investment in maintaining the status quo, and the ego operates on the principle that familiarity is best. To the ego, the unknown and unfamiliar are unsafe.

EGO DEVELOPMENT

As we adapt to family and culture, our ego and all its functions develop. The sense of self develops long before the ego or ego defense mechanisms, but the ego functions and defense mechanisms develop to enhance the sense of self further and to assist our self-in-process in adapting to each critical point of separation.

Belief systems develop as we interact with our environments. They were based on the reality of what we perceived at the time the belief systems took hold. The ego firmly established those core belief systems so that we would be safe and out of danger. Some of these belief systems serve us well, but others limit and defeat us. Thus, when we attempt to disturb the core belief systems, the ego reverts to the old "there and then" survival mode which, in the "here and now," may no longer be appropriate.

The ego also regulates other everyday functions such as thinking, learning, language, memory, intuition, comprehension, concept formation, verbal fluency, planning, anticipation, certain other phases of motor development, and our ability to make sense of things.

An ego that does its job is gently incorporated into the *self-in-process*. When the ego is in the process of adapting to a world that feels alien or hostile, it is always *on watch* and interferes with the self-in-process. In this sense, the ego defense mechanisms are the ego functions that stop progress.

> Hank was shamed as a child whenever he expressed any feelings that contradicted his parents' opinion. He became co-dependent and told them only the things they wanted to hear. When he got married, he had great difficulty expressing his feelings or being assertive. Whenever he thought there was a hint of criticism, he would become complimentary to his wife or promise to do things for her. But the obsequious behavior that had worked for him as a child was no longer appropriate, and almost ruined his marriage. His old belief system (I am powerful only if I have no feelings of my own, and I must make you happy--at any cost) reasserted itself when his old feelings of shame returned.

When Hank was a child, this defensive tactic enabled him to survive. Now, as an adult, this tactic is inappropriate and only hinders his growth toward intimacy with his wife.

Our ego's defense mechanisms keep us from looking clearly at our repetitive patterns of behavior, and at what causes the incongruence between internal and external reality. Before the discussion of ego defense mechanisms in Chapter 10 we will look at various levels of self-disclosure, in chapter 8, based on how free we feel in our world. In Chapter 9 we wll discuss the purpose of ego defense mechansism and why we use them so readily.

AWARENESS: THE JOHARI WINDOW

"All unhealthy shame is rooted in deceit of one sort or another. Bad people deceive themselves when they feel like virtuous people. Good people deceive themselves when they feel worse than they are. Either way, our feelings are out of synch with reality. However, it is hard to catch ourselves in the act of self-deceit. Nobody sets out to lie to himself; no one I know gets up in the morning and says to himself, 'I think I shall tell myself a whopper of a lie today.' The moment he lies to himself, he swears it is the truth."

—Lewis B. Smedes

"To reveal myself openly &
honestly takes the rawest
kind of courage."
—John Powell

Our level of self-disclosure depends on how safe we feel with our self and how safe we feel with others, how secretive we have been taught to be, and how blind we are to our own functioning. Seeing our belief systems clearly and changing them if we choose, depends on the openness with which we are able to be in our world.

In the 1950s two psychologists, Joe Luft and Harry Ingham, created a graphic model to illustrate how our level of healthy self-disclosure depends on a balance between what we are aware of within ourselves and are willing to share and what others are aware of about us and are willing to share. Luft and Ingham contracted their two first names and called the model the JoHari Window. [47]

Figure 5
The Johari Window

	Known to Self	Not Known to Self
Known to Others	**I** Open	**II** Blind
Not Known to Others	**III** Hidden	**IV** Unconscious

In this model, Quadrant I, the Area of Free Activity, refers to behavior and motivations known to self and known to others. If I tell you that my favorite color is yellow, then that information about me is in Quadrant I, the area of free information, known openly to both of us. Quadrant I contains information and behavior that we feel safe about and are free to share or to have known about us. The size of this quadrant may vary in different groups or situations. With my husband, this area is as large as it can be for me, because I trust him completely and feel very safe with sharing everything about my self with him. With my clients, this area is smaller, not because I do not trust them, but because my personal life is not appropriate for discussion in our client-centered relationship.

Quadrant II, the Blind Area, includes things that others can know about us but that we are not yet aware of such as habits, mannerisms, defense mechanisms, flight strategies, avoidances, and denials. These are parts of ourselves of which we are not aware, but which other people tend to see rather clearly. These areas usually get in the way of our effective functioning, because they are defenses that we erected early in life in order to survive, and we are not presently aware. These defenses served a purpose at one time but do so no longer, and therefore they get in the way of our progress toward more productive lives.

If you tell me that all my clothes and that most of my home furnishings are yellow, and I hadn't been aware of the penchant, then I was blind to that information about my yellow preference, although it was obvious to you. Once you tell me and I see the abundance of yellow, the area of information that is known to both of us is greater, and my blind spot about the color yellow is gone.

> My friend told me that I am edgy and curt when I talk to her before I go to conferences on psychodiagnostics. I was totally unaware of being irritated. Once she told me, I became aware of that feeling. She was right! This edginess was no longer in my blind area.

Quadrant III, the Hidden or Avoided Area, represents things we know but do not reveal to others (for example, a hidden agenda, or matters about which we have sensitive feelings). It includes those feelings and dreams that we "dare not" disclose for whatever reason. It includes those things that we believe should not be discussed or felt because our parents or early significant others thought they were secrets. An example would be attitudes about discussing money, which is taboo in some families. I had a client who felt that a friend who asked how much he paid for rent was prying and invading his privacy. Many people feel that the amount of money they make each month, or how they come by their money, belongs in Quadrant III.

Certainly there are areas of ourselves that we want to keep private. There may be things we prefer not want to share even with our closest friends. These thoughts and feelings may be fleeting or deeply-embedded in our consciousness, but we fear they might influence someone's feelings about us or that others might criticize us or laugh at us, or that something we reveal might be used against us. These are areas in which we feel that not sharing is safer than sharing, and not revealing ourselves saves us from hurt. Phrases such as "People in glass houses shouldn't throw stones," and "If you can't say something nice, don't say anything at all" are rationalizations that come from trying to keep hidden what we want to hide.

There is good reason not to reveal *everything* about ourselves in every situation. In my psychotherapy groups, if a new member begins to reveal too much in the first meeting it is my job to intercede. The dynamics of the group are such that if the revelations are not stopped, the other group members will tend to oust that member and *refuse* to deal with him or her for a number of sessions. [48] Timing of revealing intimate details is very important. Sudden revelation about certain parts of ourselves seems to be unacceptable. Asking someone to know about us seems to need a foundation. On the other hand, research supports that we often keep things to ourselves because we do not accurately perceive the supportive behavior of others. We often wear masks *to protect ourselves.*

If for some reason I was ashamed about my favorite color and I only wore my yellow clothes in private, the subject of my favorite color would be in Quadrant III. If you mentioned the color yellow to me, I might even deny that I liked it.

> I was seeing a couple for marriage counseling, and I sensed that there might be a problem with their sex life. When I asked them about it, the husband said, "It's fine." The wife looked down at the carpet. I pressed the issue a bit further and the husband said that he would never discuss such a thing with a third party. It was too private and none of anyone

else's business. Their sex life, at least for the husband, was in Quadrant III.

Quadrant IV, the Area of Unknown Activity, is where neither the individual nor others are aware of certain behaviors or motives. Yet we can assume their existence because eventually some of these behaviors and motives influence relationships. It is the area that is wholly unconscious to ourselves and unknown to others. It might include the area in which we dream. It is the area in which most of our belief systems are *couched*. The definition of *to couch* is particularly important to consider in this context: *To lie in ambush or concealment; to lurk; to be in a heap or pile as leaves for decomposition or fermentation.* The unconscious area is where our belief systems live, hidden and lying in ambush to keep us from change and "danger." Traumas and hypnotic events such as our parents yelling at us when we were little children get locked in the unconscious area. At that moment we were traumatized, and whatever transgression invited the yelling got locked inside of us, where it can determine behavior later in our lives.

"What it is, I don't know captain.
It's in Quadrant IV!"

If our parent is upset at dinner and yells at us for the way we are eating or the amount we are eating, we might incorporate that everything given must be eaten. "Clean your plate," "Remember the starving children in China," and "Finish that or you won't get any more," were demands made on some of my clients who have eating disorders today.

What is most important is that, the fewer hidden and blind areas there are in our lives, the smaller the unconscious area becomes.

Figure 6
Possible Variations in Levels of Self-Disclosure

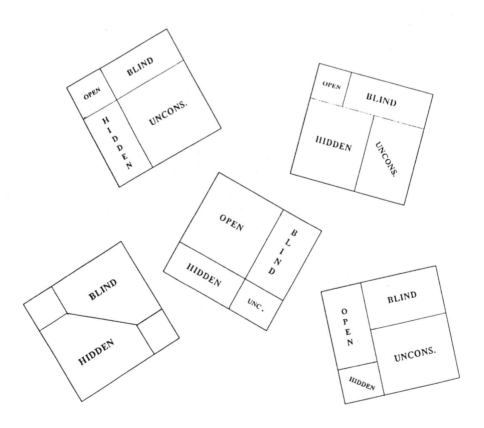

PRINCIPLES OF CHANGE

1. A change in any one quadrant will affect all other quadrants. When we can feel safe enough to tell someone about an area that we had previously hidden, then the hidden area is smaller and the area of open activity is larger.

> At a party recently we were playing the *Ungame*. One of the questions was "Tell a wish that you have not shared with these people." Our friend paused a long time and then said, with tears in her eyes, "I want another baby but Dan doesn't want the trouble." This moment of revelation made us forget about the game. Dan talked about his feelings and Cathy talked about hers. We listened empathetically. Our group of friends became closer and more open. The area of *hidden information* was reduced.

2. It takes energy to hide, deny, or be blind to behavior that is involved in interaction. There is a saying, "If you're going to lie, you have to have a great memory." If you lie, you have to remember to whom you said what. Remembering takes energy. It also takes energy to feel *out of sync* in our relationships. When we feel inside the way that we are understood outside, we feel a sense of peace. I call this *feeling congruent*. One of the most painful feelings in the world is to feel misunderstood. When we hide, deny, or are blind to our behavior or feelings, we are vulnerable to being misunderstood and having people react to us in ways we do not understand.

3. Threat tends to decrease awareness. Mutual trust tends to increase awareness. In fact, when someone exposes us without our permission or willing participation, the area of free activity will become smaller, because our trust level will decrease. We will tend to become more guarded and more superficial with the person we feel betrayed us.

4. Forced awareness (exposure) is undesirable and usually ineffective.

5. The smaller the area of free activity (Quadrant I), the poorer the communication.

6. There is a universal curiosity about the unknown area; but this is held in check by custom, social training, and by diverse fears.

7. Sensitivity means appreciating the covert aspects of behavior in Quadrants II, III, and IV, and respecting the desire of others to keep them covert. [49]

8. Blind areas are kept blind by defensiveness.

9. Hidden areas are kept hidden by defensiveness.

**Bill was proud he got his blinders, ear muffs and shield up first.
The perfect defense before Mary attacks.**

Discovering what belief systems are and discriminating between healthy belief systems and belief systems that are limiting or self-defeating is the task of the self-in-process. We need to feel good about who we are and to whom we *tell all.* On the other hand, it takes energy to keep things hidden or blind. Is it worth it to hide or not know essential things that would allow us to grow?

The rewards of self-disclosure are: Increased self-knowledge, closer intimate relationships, improved communication, fewer and lighter guilt feelings, and more energy. 50

APPRECIATING INTERPERSONAL COMMUNICATIONS

When we believe that freer interpersonal communication is of value, then we learn, often in penetrating and meaningful ways, to understand ourselves better in terms of our own ideas, feelings, and behavior. We come to appreciate to a greater extent the richness of interpersonal relationships which, up until now, may have seemed routine or threatening. Increasing our awareness of how we perceive the world in comparison to

the feedback we receive from others and

how others perceive the world in contrast to how we
perceive the world

will improve our personal incongruence. In this process of curiosity and openness, the need for defensiveness can be reduced or eliminated. We are free to be more of what we can be, what we really want to be and more of who we are.

Progress toward a greater area of free activity comes from less of a need to hide ourselves and less of a need to defend ourselves from the feedback that will open our blind areas. The option of not defending ourselves, not needing to wear masks or use facades, leads to an openness and flexibility of thought. This openness and flexibility of thought leads us to a fuller repertoire of options and greater freedom to behave in ways that previous personal inhibitions may have prevented.

EGO DEFENSE MECHANISMS
THAT KEEP US FROM CHANGING

"To bring your mode of self-destructiveness
to conscious awareness is to remove a hidden block
to the expression of your true shining nature."
—Alan Cohen

"The difference between a flower and a weed is a judgement."
—Barry Neil Kaufman

Major forms of ego defense mechanism are denial, rationalization and displacement. Definitions of these and other defense mechanisms will be given in the next chapter. These examples show how strong ego defense mechanisms are in preventing change.

DENIAL

After six years of occupying the same offices, Doris suddenly lost her major client and could not pay the rent. When the property manager came by for the rent, Doris felt acute anxiety, dizzy and sick to her stomach. Her whole world seemed to be crumbling around her.

For days Doris went over and over the problem. She felt ashamed that she could not live up to her agreements. Despite her MBA and seventeen successful years in business, Doris ruminated, "I am a poor manager, I'm not mature enough to fend for myself. I wish I had just gone to work for my family's business. Then, my mother would be responsible. She's the one who really knows how to handle money."

When a threat is perceived where there is none, or a threat is perceived as being greater than it actually is, you can tell that a core belief has surfaced.

Doris' core belief was that failure in any endeavor meant she was worthless. Her family had always treated her as an inept child, even though she had been successful at work for almost two decades. When she finally had failed, by not being able to pay rent, her ego had to put up a defense so she did not *fall apart*.

Doris went into denial, a defense that allowed her to cope with her extreme anxiety. She convinced herself that the property manager would probably not come. And, she did not prepare to move.

"I'm such a small company, in such a large building. They probably will let me stay for the term of my lease."

After a few months, the building owner served her with eviction papers. She was *shocked* by their *unfair action*. Completely unprepared, Doris had to throw things in boxes at the last minute, barely able to get out before the marshal came to padlock the office door.

94

RATIONALIZATION

Sarah is losing her sight due to sugar diabetes. She is addicted to sugar and she used to buy a candy bar every day on her way home from work. As her eyesight worsened, she promised herself that she would not buy any more candy. She then began stealing the candy and rationalized that since she wasn't buying it, it didn't count. Sarah's rationalization may cause blindness.

DISPLACEMENT

When Sister Mary called me in 1972 to ask me to be principal of a Roman Catholic school, my first thought was, *I'm not a nun.* What I did not know was that the Roman Catholic Church, under the aegis of Pope John, had changed the rules. The nuns who used to eat in private, wear traditional garb, travel only with other nuns, and cover their heads with veils were no longer restricted. They could wear secular clothes, go to the hairdresser, eat and travel alone and where they chose. In addition, since there were fewer women entering the convents, some of the Roman Catholic schools were closing, and others were turned over to lay principals. I accepted the position to serve as the school's administrative head, thinking that I would be working with the nuns who had taught me and whom I revered. To my shock and surprise, the job was quite difficult, due to the resistance and resentment from the nuns. (One nun refused to give me the accounting books because she felt I would sell the names of the donors of the school to a mailing list!) Years later, upon reflection, I can see that the nuns displaced their anger and feelings of abandonment by the church on to me.

Nancy Myer Hopkins discusses the reaction of parishioners to the disclosure that a minister/priest sexually molested a child in the parish. The expression of the anger was displaced into the following situations:

One congregation added on to their church building, and they were fighting over whether or not to have an altar rail. The congregation had never really processed the offending pastor's behavior as it became public after he had left. The altar rail fight symbolized the issue of setting boundaries between the parishioners and ministers. People were reported to align themselves in that fight according to how well they were able to accept the news of their former pastor's behavior.

In another case, the church sponsored a child-care center, but kept the children and the staff literally locked in the basement with access to the upstairs barred. The staff of the school said they felt like the congregation's bastard child, and the *after pastor* stated that...*they were taking on the shame for the congregation.*

In another case, a large urban congregation fought bitterly over how they were going *to dispose of their garbage.* 51

ANXIETY

When our well-being is threatened in any way, we feel anxious. Anxiety is a physiological sensation labeled as *uncomfortable* or *nervous,* the experience of *worry, dread, fear,* or *apprehension.* In extreme situations we can have *anxiety attacks* which are so powerful and severe that we feel as if we were having a heart attack. The feeling of this type of anxiety is intolerable. Clients I know who have experience *anxiety attacks* say that "dying would be easier." One client described the onset of an attack as an "overall foggy feeling where all thoughts seem non-existent, when the pains in my chest feel like a tightness that will squeeze the life out of me."

Anxiety can come from many sources. The causes of anxiety that are relevant to the self-in-process are the ones to which we respond defensively and the ones that cause us to feel helpless. When a core belief system is threatened, especially if it has to do with our basic familiar style, we feel anxious. When our belief systems are questioned, we feel anxious because our security feels threatened. These belief systems were formed as a result of a trauma when our safety needs were primary. (See Maslow's Hierarchy of Needs in Chapter 2).

Howard cannot admit to hostile feelings toward his abusive father. Anger at his parent is in direct conflict with his core belief system: "A good son loves his father no matter what." To confront his father in any way produces anxiety because it threatens his feeling of being loved and feeling like a good son. Howard feels anxious when he thinks about confronting his father. He feels he is *doing something wrong* and must use some method to stop the anxiety. The most common method of stopping the anxiety is to stop the angry feelings and defend the *goodness* of his father. This behavior enables him to comfort himself with the belief that he is a good son and to feel that he belongs.

Another cause of anxiety is feeling helpless and out of control. If we learn that we cannot trust our environment, we are in a state of constant anxiety because every situation we find ourselves in is a potential threat. We feel ambiguous about even good situations because of our mistrust. We do not feel OK so we are constantly cautious and vigilant. This feeling is sometimes called *free-floating anxiety*.

**"He's either in the flight part of fight or
just experiencing basic free-floating anxiety."**

Lynn and Brent had been married for five years when he decided he wanted a divorce. She was shocked and felt devastated. She agreed to do anything to change herself, to help him--anything to save the marriage. He agreed that "she was perfect in every way except he no longer was romantically in love with her. He wanted a divorce." She pleaded with him, "I will do anything to change your mind, just tell me what to do." He assured her that there was "nothing for her to do because it had nothing to do with her." She developed a *free-floating* anxiety and was unable to work, eat, or sleep. She was out of control.

DEALING WITH ANXIETY

There are two ways of dealing with the anxiety: The *self-in-process* is able to examine the core belief system to determine if it is healthy or unhealthy and see if the belief is still appropriate. Does Howard's anger at his father mean he is a bad son? Does Lynn really want to be married to a man who does not love her?

The other, less healthy way to deal with anxiety is to dispel it through defense mechanisms. Howard can deny his anger toward his father for the abuse. Howard can rationalize that his father was abusive because Howard was a "bad kid." Lynn can blame Brent for abandoning her. Lynn can displace her anger at Brent onto feeling unattractive and depressed.

Defense mechanisms can be adaptive, healthy and in service of the self-in-process. They may allow us to distort reality momentarily, to tolerate trauma until we can more directly handle it. Defense mechanisms, in general, however, are out of our awareness and limit our development.

Our ego defense mechanisms serve to ensure our feelings of security and to prevent anxiety. The ego defense mechanisms operate at an unconscious level and are more or less automatic. All defense mechanisms distort reality in some way. Defense mechanisms are formed when we feel the overwhelming demand to respond to circumstances over which we have no control.

When we are children, defense mechanisms serve to ward off anxiety caused by feeling we are "bad" when we do not feel loved, when our needs are inconsistently taken care of, or when we are overwhelmed by what we think we must do in order to survive. We develop strategies to defend against what feels like annihilation, disapproval, rejection, humiliation or loss of love.

Annihilation is an important concept to understand. Annihilation is the process of utter destruction, being completely destroyed, of being reduced to nonexistence. 52

> Not long ago I was washing an expensive crystal goblet we received as a wedding present. It slipped out of my hand and hit the sink shattering in what seemed to be a million pieces. It was utterly gone. It had been annihilated. All the pieces that made it a goblet were there, but the essence was gone. "It" could no longer be referred to as a goblet.

The emotional experience of being abandoned feels like breaking into tiny, unrecognizable pieces. The force *within us to avoid* this feeling is *extremely powerful.*

"You know if I didn't have doubts, shames, mistrusts, guilts, fears, longings, fear of failures, tensions, anxieties, I could have potential."

99

THE PURPOSE OF EGO DEFENSE MECHANISMS

Ego defense mechanisms have many purposes. Their primary purpose is to avoid feeling unloved and annihilated. Defense mechanisms are not healthy when they substitute for reality. They are also an inefficient way to meet our needs, because the underlying cause for the defense mechanism remains intact and takes energy away from healthy functioning.

My purpose in discussing the defense mechanisms is not to put labels on our behavior, but rather to begin to recognize the defense mechanisms that we use to maintain the underlying *belief systems.*

Every ego has a *favorite* method of defending itself. The ego defense mechanisms we use are related to *the ones that work* or the way others in our immediate family have used them. If our family denies the reality of a situation, then we learn to deny reality also. If our family displaces anger from inside the family to outside the family, then we begin displacing our anger at family members onto playmates, teachers, or our next-door neighbor. If we hear rationalizations as a viable excuse for our behavior, then we use rationalizations too.

The defense mechanisms stop growth, which we exchange for security. Using the defense mechanisms, however, delays or magnifies the *issue* we need to face to free ourselves from limiting or self-defeating *belief systems.* Becoming aware of defense mechanisms is the first step. Once we recognize them, we will have a choice about whether or not to use, rather than deal with issues as they arise.

Discovering our defense mechanisms is not easy because they are not readily available for direct examination. Most defense mechanisms fall in the blind or unconscious areas of the Johari Window. Some may be quite obvious to others. Others may be out of our awareness and the awareness of others.

Our job is to become aware of our own defenses so we have the choice to make a genuine lasting change.

DEFINITIONS OF EGO DEFENSE MECHANISMS

"'Sorry, but that is the way I am...
I was like this in the beginning, am now, and ever shall be..."
is a handy motto and delusion to have around you
if you don't want to grow up."
—John Powell

"I've learned that it's OK when your best
isn't good-enough, but not being good-enough
does not justify a defense."
—Alice Vieira

This chapter discusses the common ego defense mechanisms we employ to keep us from real feelings, confrontations, and most unfortunately, *awareness*.

SUBLIMATION

This socially acceptable defense happens when an acceptable need is substituted for an unacceptable one. A child who enjoys seeing blood may become a surgeon. A child who needs an excessive amount of attention may become an actor.

Mary began lying about what happened to her during the day. She would fabricate the day's events until her mother could not believe anything she said, and had to call teachers or her playmates to find out when events were actually taking place. Mary's teacher suggested that Mary begin writing her stories for a little book that would be read to the class at the end of each day. Mary's need to create stories was sublimated into a creative endeavor.

Billy always disturbed his parents' friends by his antics while they were visiting. He would tumble through the room or bang loudly on his drum when his parents had guests. When he was given the attention he craved, he would seem pleased for days. Billy sublimated his need for attention into becoming a very successful actor.

When I was 14 I fell "in love" for the first time. One evening I was talking about Johnny, age 17, to my parents, and began describing these special feelings I had when I thought about him. My father calmly suggested that Johnny and I find some physical activities that we could do together--such as tennis or hiking--to use up energy that was natural but inappropriate at this time. That seemed reasonable to me. (It didn't seem reasonable to Johnny!)

DENIAL

This is a mechanism of defense in which obvious real factors are treated as if they did not exist. For one reason or another we find certain external factors painful, and we literally deny their presence. I often see clients who disregard all kinds of clues suggesting that their spouse is having an affair, because the pain of acknowledging that reality would be intolerable.

> Al, now age 62, is a retired computer programmer who lives alone. When he was 30 he had married a woman with four children. Al and his wife had a son, whom they named after Al's best friend Peter. A few months after little Pete's birth, Al found his wife in bed with Peter. Al immediately divorced his wife and disowned little Pete--denying paternity. But Al's parents continued a long, endearing relationship with little Pete, whom they very much considered their grandchild, and had pictures of them (the grandparents) and Pete. At a family gathering these pictures were being shown around. Al said, "Isn't amazing how much Chip (a cousin present at the gathering) still looks the same." Of the 30 people present, Al was the only person who did not recognize Pete and no one told Al that the picture was of his own son.

This is a good example of how we respect another person's need to remain in the dark. When there is more denial, there is more blind area, and less possibility of change.

> Erik, age 35, the owner of a large furniture outlet store, had become a millionaire at 25. He worked 100 hours per week. When his wife told him she had been having an affair and wanted a divorce, he had a stroke. The doctor told him he would never walk again. Erik told his doctor that was ridiculous! that there was no way that he could carry on his business from bed. The doctor laughed, but within two months Erik was up and walking and indeed was back carrying on business as usual.

Sometimes *denial* is essential to survive. Studies that show that young children who deny that they have a terminal illness, survive longer and are more likely to go into remission than those children not in denial. On the other hand, women who deny that they have a lump in their breast out of fear that it "might be cancer" and refuse to consult a doctor may die unnecessarily.

I see numerous divorced clients who cannot face the fact that they can no longer depend on a spouse they had planned to live with their entire life. They still look to the spouse for approval (or continued disapproval), for direction and support. Their *denial* keeps them from moving on with their life.

There are ways to recognize being in denial:

☐ Defending our family of origin.

☐ Speaking in generalities: "No one had it great." "All families have problems." "We were Italian."

☐ Refusing to acknowledge that our parents influenced our lives.

☐ Taking full responsibility for "the way I am."

☐ Having no feelings about our family one way or the other.

☐ Never allowing any anger.

☐ Feeling superior to our parents.

☐ Purporting "I can do it myself--I am responsible for the way I am." "They did the best they could." [53]

DISPLACEMENT

Displacement is a defense mechanism through which the emotion that was initially attached to one person or situation is displaced to another person or situation, that is less threatening. As with other mechanisms of defense, the defense is needed to prevent distress. The emotion is, therefore, displaced onto a less threatening situation or person, and the original situation is relegated to the unconscious. A popular example of this mechanism is the man who comes home and kicks the dog after a bad day at the office.

> Delores is a 24-year-old single parent of a five-year-old. She had been dating George for two years and, although they were living together, they were not married. When Delores got pregnant, she pressed George to marry her. He refused and walked out of the house. Delores turned to her five-year-old and began yelling at her for not picking up her toys, for being messy, and told her to go to her room until she could be a decent child. Delores displaced her frustration, hurt, and anger onto her child.

Freud suggested that displacement of aggressive or sexual impulses may be healthy: Aggressive and sexual impulses may be displaced into boxing or other competitive sports. My father suggested tennis and hiking for me when I was 14 and had feelings for Johnny.

IDENTIFICATION

Identification is an unconscious process of taking into ourselves a mental picture of something or someone, and then thinking, feeling, and acting as we imagine that thing or person would think, feel or act. A powerful example, often cited, is that of prisoners of war.

Prisoners who *identified* with captors became cruel and controlling of other prisoners. Bruno Bettelheim described insidious camp experiences during World War II. "A prisoner had reached the final stage of adjustment to the camp situation when he had changed his personality so as to accept as his own the values of the Gestapo....old prisoners were sometimes instrumental in getting rid of the unfit, in this way making a feature of Gestapo ideology a feature of their own behavior." [54] This is called "identification with the aggressor."

HEROES

A less dramatic example is how we identify with our heroes. We like to think and feel the way we believe someone we admire thinks and feels. The people we copy or imitate mold our personality. We look for mentors and role models with whom we identify. When we identify with our parents, for example, we adopt their values and loyalties as our own. This identification serves to make criticism of them impossible because we *believe the same thing*. The fact that over 70 percent of us remain in the same political party as our parents, is only one example of how this defense mechanism manifests itself. Changing to a political party different from that of our parents can become a major issue, if it can be done at all.

"You know, I was hoping you
would tell me what it is."

"I have waited so many
years. Oh great one,
tell me the meaning of life?"

We need heroes so that we can have someone to admire. The need reveals a longing for a father figure: "The decisiveness of thought, the strength of will, the forcefulness of his deeds, belong to the picture of the father; above all other things, however, the self-reliance and independence of the great man, his divine conviction of doing the right thing, which may pass into ruthlessness. He must be admired, he may be trusted, but one cannot help also being afraid of him." [55]

Years ago it was easy to identify the heroes in the movies: John Wayne, Gary Cooper in *High Noon, The Lone Ranger, Superman.* In the late sixties and early seventies, Astronauts filled the hero-bill. John Kennedy, also a hero because of his youth, his image, his sense of humor and quick-wittedness with the press, instituted the physical fitness programs that led the nation to identify with astronauts by paying attention to fitness and physical exercise.

As families we identified with *Father Knows Best, Ozzie and Harriet,* the *Brady Bunch* and other models on television. As women, we had fewer female heroes, but we identified with "the hero who would take care of us." Today kids buy Nike shoes to be "like" Michael Jordan. An excellent example of a woman identifying with the late Jacqueline Kennedy Onassis was portrayed by the Michelle Pffeifer character in the movie *Love Fields.* She wore her hair like Jackie, and when she described losing her baby, she said she lost it "like Jackie Kennedy did."

It is common for children to identify (to want to be like) with the same-sex parent. This is different from the attachment we have to the opposite-sexed parent.

Identification becomes more than imitation of the same-sexed parent. We respond as if we were that parent. We, as children, feel as though we are the recipient of a reward if our parent receives a reward. We feel hurt and disappointed if we see our parents hurt or disappointed. We also use siblings, peers, teachers, and TV or movie characters as role models and mentors who *teach* us new responses.

Exaggerating the strength, importance, and wealth of our family becomes a common means of enhancing our own prestige. I can remember telling my little friend, Mary, that if my father wanted to, he could lift up our house." We also begin to evaluate ourselves in light of our group identifications. College students feel elated when their team wins and say, "We won!" They feel dejected if, "We got trounced!" Parents often identify with their children's accomplishments and defeats.

When we have closely identified with our parents' political party, societal class or culture, it can seem as much a part of us as our name or gender. Changing strong identifications shakes our very foundation.

INTROJECTION

Introjection is a defense mechanism by which we take in and *swallow whole* certain human characteristics or traits in order to gain control of them in some way. This defense mechanism is particularly important when we are children and assume the "standards and mores" of our parents, without ever questioning what, in actuality, is right or wrong for us.

Introjection is a way to hold on to a loved person or thing when a threatened loss or separation is felt. Again, the greater the abuse, the greater the attachment to the loved person, and therefore the greater the introjection.

Introjection differs from identification. In identification we recognize that we are "like Barbra Streisand" by copying her hair style, imitating her clothes, etc. With introjection, we may take on Barbra's traits without any awareness that we are "like her."

> My friend's husband died, and at his funeral she began drinking lots of water, which was unusual for her. Later she remembered that her husband always drank lots of water. She had introjected his water-drinking habit into herself as a way of not letting go of him.

"In revolutions leading to dictatorial forms of government, many people introject the new values and beliefs as a protection against behavior that might get them into trouble."

"Introjection is thus a defensive reaction which seems to follow the general idea, *if you can't beat 'em, join 'em.*" Apparently, from an ego-defensive point of view, it is better to be good or bad oneself than to be continually at the mercy of good or bad objects or forces from without." 56

ISOLATION

Isolation is a defense mechanism in which an incident, and the emotions associated with it, become separated. The emotions remain unconscious, while the incident is allowed into consciousness. This defense mechanism allows us to remember an incident without feeling the pain of the incident.

> A woman client described, somewhat light-heartedly, watching her daughter die after removal of life supports. She had separated the agony of those moments from the sequence of events as she described them to me.

It is not uncommon for people to discuss painful incidents with a smile interspersed with laughter.

PHOBIAS

Phobias are unrealistic fears placed on non-threatening persons or things. More and more I listen to men and women who have exaggerated fears about relationships. Steve Carter, in his book *Men Who Can't Love*, refers to the men he writes about as commitment-phobic. 57

> Donald had been emotionally abused by his parents. He was afraid to tell them what he wanted, because that would assure him he would not get whatever it was. By age 35 Donald had had numerous women in his life. The best illustration of his commitment phobia was when he took his girlfriend to a motel when he was 21 and she was 19. She undressed in

the bathroom in preparation for the romantic evening, emerging from the little room in a negligee and soft robe. He, being a bit uncomfortable, glanced down at her bare feet and noticed that she had particularly tiny toes. He felt immediately turned off, so he left her, and the motel, without saying a word.

For a commitment-phobic person, any reason to avoid a deepening relationship will be sufficient to end it. Most commitment-phobics begin their "scan" to end the relationship within seconds of meeting a new person.

When Steve was 15, he was told he had to leave his house because he refused to continue to be what he called the "Cinderella-boy slave." He was on his own too early. He longed to belong, but he also feared that he would be mistreated if he ever let go of having complete control. He married a woman who was "not up to his standards" but one he felt he could mold and fix. In the first two years of their marriage, she conformed to most of his demands, and when she didn't he would belittle her as his mother had belittled him. After they had a baby, his wife matured and resented his continued attempt to control her. He felt that what he was *teaching* her to do was reasonable, and that she needed to *obey* him. But after a year of couples' therapy, he still would not relinquish his criticism of her and her ways. Now Steve is divorced and has begun to date. He found a woman with whom he had lots of fun. He enjoyed her companionship and felt he was falling in love with her, but knew that he could not continue to love her because she did not have a voluptuous body. He told her that her figure did not appeal to him. In both instances, Steve was avoiding commitment to a relationship--not to an imperfect body.

I believe that people are terrified of relationships because they are attached so completely to their abusive parents--the greater the abuse, the greater the attachment. They displace anxiety about being abandoned by their parents, or the anxiety about abandoning their parents, by creating checklists that are impossible for potential mates to fulfill. They remain available to parents and unavailable to a marital commitment.

Janet is a 40 year-old only child who has never been married and is the focus of her unhappily-married parents. In therapy, Janet began to realize how much of her life she was giving up for her parents. Janet began to limit her phone calls to two or three times per month instead of several times per week. She shared fewer details of her life with them. She talked to a male friend of hers and suggested that they pursue "more than a friendship," indicating that they would add sexual intimacy and "see what would develop." Janet did not tell her parents about Lenny, and she didn't tell them what she was doing in as much detail. Within weeks she received a card (meant for a little child) from her father saying, "When you were born, you gave meaning to our lives--which meant nothing without you." The message seemed to be, "If you abandon me, I will die." Janet then displaced her frustration and anger at her parents' manipulation. Her boyfriend suddenly seemed boring and unattractive, and she felt irritated and angry with him. She felt closer to her parents and began calling them more often.

PROJECTION

Projection is a defense mechanism whereby painful or objectionable emotions are thrown out onto other persons or things. It is a way of making something unacceptable in ourselves visible in someone else, so we can deal with it outside ourselves. If I hate myself, I may project this inner hate onto others and feel that they hate me.

Jerry always feels he is being cheated, when, in reality, it is he who "tries to get something for nothing" by not wanting to pay the going wage for services provided him. Jerry calls the plumber or gardener "a highway robber" for charging fees that are considered appropriate.

A former mayor of a town in Southern California town opposed pornography and fought hard to get it off the streets, condemning and jailing participants. It was later found out that he owned one of the largest pornographic film and video collections in America.

111

**The next time Jack projected on to her,
Janet promised to get his attention with finger puppets.**

RATIONALIZATION

Rationalization is a defense mechanism in which we attempt to prove that our behavior is *rational* and justifiable, and thus worthy of self and social approval. Rationalization utilizes two major defense values:
(1) It helps us to justify what we do and what we believe and (2) It aids us in softening the disappointment connected with unattainable goals. 58

Rationalization is a way of substituting an acceptable reason for an unacceptable one, in order to explain a given action or attitude. We rationalize by "inventing" a reason for an action when we prefer not to recognize the true motive. Rationalization is almost synonymous with justification.

A woman eating chocolate cake when her weight-conscious friend visits might say (justifying it to herself as well), "Oh, I'm so hungry that I had to grab something quick!"

My favorite example of rationalization is when a client explained using marijuana "as a homeopathic remedy." He explained that with marijuana there are grades in the alteration of consciousness, so that half a hit off a mild marijuana cigarette helped him work better, but did not make him high.

A good example from history that illustrates how complicated rationalizations can be, comes from Benjamin Franklin's autobiography:

I believe I have omitted mentioning that, in my first voyage from Boston, being becalmed off Block Island, our people set about catching cod, and hauled up a great many. Hitherto I had stuck to my resolution of not eating animal food, and on this occasion considered with my Master, the taking of every fish as a kind of unprovoked murder, since none of them had, or ever could do us any injury that might justify the slaughter. All this seemed very reasonable. But I had formerly been a great lover of fish, and, when this came hot out of the frying pan, it smelt admirably well. I balanced some time between principle and inclination, till I recollected that, when the fish were opened, I saw smaller fish taken out of their stomachs; then thought I," If you eat one another, I don't see why we mayn't eat you." So I dined upon cod very heartily and continued to eat it with other people, returning only now and then occasionally to a vegetable diet. So convenient a thing it is to be a reasonable creature, since it enables one to find or make a reason for everything one has a mind to do. 59

REACTION FORMATION

Reaction Formation is a defense mechanism which results in a rigid attitude or character trait, to govern or prevent the emergence of a painful or undesirable attitude or trait. That attitude or character trait is frequently the opposite of the one we hope to avoid. A man, whose father is self-centered in the eyes of most people, becomes the "nicest guy in town" by going out of his way to be generous, thoughtful and selfless. This man may be described as having a reaction to being self-centered.

For the same reason it is not uncommon for a preacher's daughter to become a prostitute.

There is a relatively new *Twelve Step group for alcoholics* who have a reaction-formation to their "old way of life," and become addicted to fundamental religious sects--condemning drinking, TV, dancing--anything they did in excess prior to their sobriety.

REGRESSION

Regression is a defense mechanism by which we abandon an achieved level of development and return to an earlier, less mature and less evolved developmental level. When the mother of a four-year-old has a new baby, the four-year-old may start to suck his thumb, want to nurse at mother's breast, and return to baby-talk.

Regression can also happen in adults, who revert to acting like children. Less pathological, and more common, is regressing to old patterns of behavior when we are under stress. I see this type of regression in my practice when clients have learned new, healthier ways of handling situations, but under great stress, they revert to the pre-therapy way of behaving.

> Trent learned to pout as a means of showing his dissatisfaction with something his wife or children did. It was what his parents did (and do) to show their disapproval. Trent learned in therapy that pouting was a passive-aggressive way to deal with problems and learned to state his disapproval in a constructive, direct manner that was received and responded to positively by his wife and children.
>
> When his business began to fail, he regressed to pouting without awareness. Once it was pointed out to him that he was pouting, he was

114

quickly able to pull himself out of that behavior. Pouting had been a safe retreat for him, but an ineffective means to get his needs met. Without the pouting, he was able to do what was needed to turn his business around.

REPRESSION

Repression is an unconscious but active process of keeping internal, unacceptable ideas from consciousness. Ideas that are unacceptable because they are in conflict with our morals, values, or self-image and may elicit extreme pain. Repression also helps control dangerous desires and minimizes the disruptive effects of painful experiences. It is often referred to as "selective forgetting." Just as denial is a defense against an external threat, repression is a defense against an internal one.

Bob represses his parents.

Repression is a mechanism that prevents us from experiencing unacceptable feelings about ourselves. The example of Howard (Chapter 9) equating anger at his father with being a bad son caused Howard to repress his anger. Repression allows us to "forget consciously" memories that are traumatic. The purpose of repression is to protect us from the threat of who we think we are, as a result of how we had to be in order to survive.

Repression requires a great deal of energy not to reveal a feeling, idea or impulse. Hatred of one's parents is often repressed. When an idea is repressed, other defense mechanisms may take over to release some of our "pent-up energy." We may displace the idea of hating our parents (which has been repressed) into hating authority figures or breaking the law (which releases our bottled-up hostility.) We may "just get sick." One client of mine comes down with a cold or flu after every visit with his mother. He describes his visits with her as "taxing--but wonderful!"

"Hey man, I've got some pent-up energy here."

Repressed energy may express itself in the form of a verbal denial of things we actually want. I had a friend who always said "No, thank you every time I asked if she wanted a piece of cake or a second helping of dinner. She would then help herself to whatever had been offered. When we say, "That's the last thing I was thinking of," we may mean it was "the first thing that came to mind."

Relief from repression does not happen automatically. We have to be willing to find out if the thoughts or ideas we had are still *horrible*. It is difficult to express feelings that we think are unacceptable. This is why we continue to carry a lot of unnecessary fears that are left over from childhood. Once awareness and reality-testing free us from repressions, the energy that is bound up in repression can be focused on more productive endeavors.

The energy that is used to repress ideas could better be used in dealing with problems that are causing the repression. Coleman says, "It is of value to distinguish repression from suppression."[60]

REPRESSION VERSUS SUPPRESSION

Suppression differs from repression in that we consciously *put an idea out of our mind*, and think of other things. Thus, it is not as dangerous to our mental health as repression is apt to be, for it is deliberate--we know what we are doing. Repression occupies space and time in our unconscious. The concept of selective forgetting may be more accurately stated as selective remembering because material that is repressed can be recalled under hypnosis or use of sodium pentothal, but not otherwise.

When I was Dean of Girls at San Gabriel High School, Rita, a beautiful 14-year-old blond, was sent to me because she was digging her pencil eraser into her hands and arms until she had bleeding holes in her skin. She told me that she hated herself and always had, but she did not know why. After months of counseling she remembered that when she was eight, her father had told her to take off the nylons she had taken from her mother's drawer, and to put on the bobby socks and saddle

117

shoes which she was supposed to wear. A terrible argument ensued and she was angrily ordered her to bed early. In her room, she cursed her father and wished him dead. Unfortunately for Rita, her father died of a heart attack that night. Since that time she had repressed that entire evening, including the fact that her current *father* was a *stepfather*. When we discovered that her father had always had a serious heart condition, she was able to accept that her unacceptable wish did not kill her father.

Rita was then able to stop mutilating herself. The death of her father and the surrounding incidents were no longer repressed. She could now actively suppress any self-destructive impulses, should any arise.

**"The difference between us Edith, is that you repress
your parents, while I suppress mine."**

UNDOING

Undoing is a defense mechanism in which we do one thing to neutralize something we have previously done (real or imaginary) that we find unacceptable.

Joey, an eight-year-old, was very close to his grandfather who often took him places and played with him almost every weekend. Joey lived around the corner from his grandfather, and when he turned seven, his grandfather taught Joey to walk to his house around the corner by himself. They played a game: "Walk out of your house, go right. Go one block and go right. First house, go right." When Joey arrived, his grandfather would say, "Right, right, right!" And pick him up to give him a hug.

When Joey's grandfather died, Joey reacted to his grandfather's death with disbelief. Then, at the funeral, he burst into tears, circling the casket several times (*to the right*) in a way that appeared he was trying to find a vantage point from which to observe his grandfather coming back to life.

After the funeral Joey was not himself, and his mother noticed that it took him an inordinate amount of time to do things around the house. The reason was that Joey would only turn right! At first Joey denied that he was doing anything different than he had ever done, but then admitted to his mother that he "worried a lot about the possibility that his father might die, and that turning right, especially in circles, was one way to prevent this from happening." Joey was trying to undo death by turning right.

Erik, the furniture store owner who had a stroke at age 35, completely denied that working 100 hours per week had anything to do with his wife's affair and their subsequent divorce. Erik attributed his stroke to stress he placed on himself by always being 10 to 15 minutes late to work--a habit he felt endangered business deals. Erik decided that he would never be late again and, after his recovery, he began arriving 10 to 15 minutes early to every appointment. He was convinced that if he was early, he would prevent another stroke.

There are a few other defenses that, although not technically considered to be ego defense mechanisms, are nevertheless significant defenses that should be considered hindrances to growth. The are *Acting Out, Acting In, and Being Unsafe*.

ACTING OUT

Acting Out is manifested in dealing with conflicts by overt behavior, rather than controlling the behavior, suppressing the impulse, or using defense mechanisms to avoid dealing with them. Acting Out is a way to avoid issues that, if resolved, would allow us to change. Acting Out is typical behavior in antisocial personalities. A dramatic example of this is Jack the Ripper. "Jack" is said to have killed numerous women to avoid dealing with the feelings of hate he felt for his mother. Acting Out is defined as the direct expression of an unconscious wish or impulse, in order to avoid being conscious of the accompanying affect. The unconscious fantasy is lived out impulsively in behavior, thus gratifying the impulse more than the prohibition against it. On a chronic level, Acting Out involves giving in to impulses in order to avoid the tension that would result from postponement of expression.

People with dependent needs take care of themselves in blatant Acting Out-- by insistent demanding. These are, psychologically speaking, the most immature patients. Their character is marked by the infantile trail of "I want what I want when I want it," even when gratification involves asocial or antisocial behavior that disregards the needs and rights of others and of society. As irresponsible people, with little investment in achievement, they may drift from job to job and are often unemployed. Addiction to tobacco, alcohol, and drugs are common. In their relationships, they are parasitic and without considerations of others. [61]

"Harry has a whole set of defense mechanisms."

Jenny, a 25-year-old school teacher, denied all feelings of anger. When she was confronted on any issue by her colleagues or family members, she would become silly, laugh and deflect feelings that were being expressed to her or her feelings toward others. Jenny Acted Out her anger instead of expressing it.

Acting Out is *self-destructive*. Although a this is dramatic example, self mutilation (cutting oneself, burning oneself, or digging the eraser head into her skin, as Rita did) serves to provide relief from an original unpleasant state. Rita said she discovered that digging the eraser into her hands and arms was the only thing that alleviated the intensely painful mental state she had no known reason for feeling. The following example is less traumatic, but not less dramatic.

Debra, a 34-year-old single mother who had been physically abused by her father and two subsequent husbands, fell in love with a gentle man who loved her and was good to her. After he brought her home from a date and left for his house, her anxiety over the thoughts that he might hurt her or leave her made her Act Out by drinking to excess until her anxiety passed.

Stuart had a pattern of "leaving the scene" when he became uncomfortable (be it at work, in a movie, with his family, or at a friend's house). No one knew where he lived, so no one could find him. He did not have a phone. Stuart would come and go mysteriously. By leaving situations impulsively and lying about the reason, he was Acting Out his impulse, instead of dealing with his anxiety. In this way of coping he felt safe--and, unfortunately, alone.

Ed owns a huge printing business. He does not have the necessary staff to cover the customer load along with the administrative needs of the store. Customers walk in the door to order printing, customers call to check on their orders, ask about services, and change orders. Ed operates *in a frantic mode*. When there is a problem, he yells at one of the salesmen or secretaries complaining that they didn't do this or that. He is abusive in his language, and he blames anyone in sight for the problem. Ed is totally unaware that he is yelling, that he blames others, or that he is abusive. Ed is Acting Out his frustrations. He is out of control without *awareness*.

Our egos form defenses which allow us to meet demands we feel unequipped to handle. They were erected so we could survive. Some defenses may be appropriate and adaptive. In the moment, they protect us (temporarily) from traumatic feelings or events that we cannot handle. If we feel safe, loved, and loveable, we should have less and less need for the protection that defense mechanisms give us. If, however, we continue to believe we are not lovable, we will feel the constant need to defend ourselves. (See Table 1) Our *self* doesn't get to be *in-process* because we are "busy protecting" a fragile, vulnerable ego, and the self-hate remains internalized.

Defenses allow us to meet demands we feel unequipped to handle:

Joey's ritual right turns allowed him to accept his grandfather's death and try to prevent his father's death.

Erik's early arrival allowed him to deal with the fear of dying or being completely disabled by another stroke.

Warren's *tough guy* front enabled him to avoid feeling inadequate for not being able to have a lasting relationship.

Al's denial of his son, Pete, was a defense against the pain he experienced in finding his wife in bed with his best friend.

In reality, all the energy expended by Joey, Erik, Warren and Al did not allow them to resolve their problems, or reserve the energy needed to resolve them. Joey will still need to grieve his grandfather's death. Erik still needs to reduce stress other than that of being late to work. Warren will have to learn how to create a lasting relationship and Al will have to express his disappointment and anger at the betrayal of his wife and best friend.

ACTING IN

Acting In is an excessive mental exercise that goes beyond the present situation to a future, unrealistic conclusion.

When Frank was getting dressed one morning, he was frustrated because he could not find a tie he liked. He thought that he should go out and buy a new tie. Then he went through the following scenario:
"If I go to the store, I will miss client calls."
"If I miss client calls, I will not make any money."
"If I can't get clients and make no money, then I will be a failure and lose my house."
"If I'm a failure, my father is right, I'm no good."

123

"I can't afford to buy a new tie."

Frank Acted In to his detriment, and deprived himself of a new tie.

The most common form of Acting In is in the telling of "Jack" stories, and what my clients have termed, "Jill" stories.

The Jack stories are *negative stories* we tell ourselves. Janette Rainwater describes a Jack story:

> Once upon a time a man driving on a little-traveled road in the desert suddenly had a flat tire. To his consternation, he realized that he had no jack to raise his car and change the tire. Then he remembered he had passed a service station about five miles back, and started walking. And thinking. "You know, way out here in the desert there are no other stations around. If the man who owns it doesn't want to be helpful, there's no other place I can go. I'm really at this guy's mercy. He could skin me good just for lending me a jack so I can change my tire. He could charge me $10...He could charge me $20...He could charge me $50, and there wouldn't be anything I could do about it because I'm just...why that S.O.B.! My God, how some people will take advantage of their fellow man!" The man arrives at the service station. The owner comes out and asked in a friendly way, "Hello, what can I do for you?" And our friend shouts, "You can take your goddammed jack and you can shove it!" [62]

"Jill" stories are the same as "Jack" stories, but we make the scenario wonderful before wonderful can happen. "Jill" stories are as destructive as "Jack" stories, because they eventually end in unrealistic expectations and disappointment.

> Michele was asked if she would go out on a blind date with a man who had seen her in a meeting and was attracted to her. He wanted to be introduced, and asked a friend of Michele's to double date. Michele agreed. Between the time she agreed to go and the actual date she mentioned that she might be moving out (to marry this man) and asked

124

if her roommate would be her maid of honor, and wondered if she should have two or three kids.

Michele *Acted In* about marrying someone and living happily ever after, before she even met the man.

BEING UNSAFE

Charles Whitfield, author of *Healing the Child Within,* summarized characteristics of "safe and unsafe" people at one of his workshops. His list of characteristics, which I have modified, include people who:

☐ Don't listen

☐ Don't hear

☐ Don't make eye contact

☐ Are rejecting, by judging

☐ Are not self--disclosing

☐ Have unclear boundaries

☐ Send mixed messages

☐ Tend to triangulate

☐ Betray others or betray us

☐ Are competitive

☐ Contrive relationship

☐ Are condescending

☐ Invalidate us

☐ Drain us. [63]

Unsafe listener

When we are in the early stages of awareness and change, we protect ourselves by being unsafe inside ourselves as well. We don't listen to others. We mis-hear others, and often misunderstand others. We judge others, and we do not self-disclose. We are secretive. Our boundaries are not clear. We send double messages and are indirect. We talk about other people instead of dealing directly with the people we are complaining about (triangulation). We are not loyal and are not supportive of our friends. We are superficial and find talking to people or having people around draining. Being unsafe is a defense mechanism that keeps us from flowing within a self-in-process.

When Gary was courting Irene, she talked about her desire to have a family. Gary listened but did not mention his aversion to having children. When they discussed birth control he told her he had a vasectomy but had frozen sperm in a sperm bank. When they got married and Irene pushed him to have a child, he was forced to tell her he never wanted children. Gary is an unsafe person because of his double messages, secretiveness and unwillingness to self-disclose.

126

Mark had cold, unempathetic parents who punished him when he "broke the rules." He didn't know what the rules were until he had broken them. As a result he made up his own stringent rules about life that restricted him in many areas. When he fell in love with a warm, loving store manager, he felt he wanted her to take care of him, but his "rule" was that he had to make more money than his wife. To be taken care of by a woman was unmasculine and unacceptable. He broke up the relationship. Mark is unsafe in himself. He cannot trust his own heart because of the judgements he made about how his life needs to be lived.

"What did you do today? You look a little sheepish."

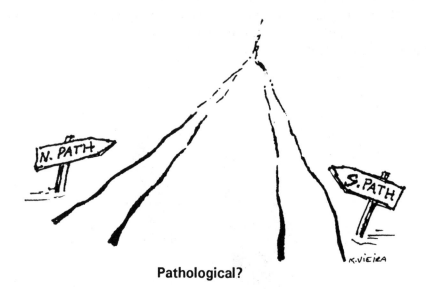

Pathological?

THE ROLE OF DEFENSE MECHANISMS IN PROHIBITING CHANGES IN BELIEF SYSTEMS

"Facts, facts are the enemy of the truth"
—Miguel Cervantes

"Nothing changes until what is becomes real"
—Frederick Perls

"Be ready for an "I" you never planned for."
—Thomas Moore

Defense mechanisms are "the means by which a person alters consciousness in order to exclude unwanted ideas, feelings or impulses." [64] Most defensiveness is unhealthy because it impairs our capacity to deal with reality and it hinders communication. When we become defensive, we react and lose our center.

CHANGES NEEDED IN DEFENSE MECHANISMS
THAT NO LONGER APPLY

During childhood, some traumatic situation may have caused a real need to defend ourself. In adulthood, this same situation may *not* be threatening at all. If, as adults, we view the world from our childhood perspective, we tend to use the same childhood defenses. These defenses fail to serve us--and instead become barriers to growth.

Heather, now 37, was raised by her defensive mother and extremely critical father. Heather was a "good kid" trying to please her parents but always falling short because of impossible or unstated standards that were set. She became defensive, Acting Out by verbally by denying any wrong doing, to avoid feeling totally inadequate. She married and had two children. When her husband or children pointed out some small mistake, like, "Mom, you forgot the jackets!" she would become defensive and attack her "accuser." Heather continued to protect herself with a defense learned in childhood, but no longer needed. Her continued use of this defensiveness hurt her present relationships with her non-critical husband and children who loved her.

Do you ever wonder why some of us can't stand any form of criticism? Our entire lives seem built on the premise that we must be right, or at least doing our best. We expect the "best" to be accepted regardless of its effects on others. This attitude is prevalent in those of us who were not mirrored or validated by our mothers or primary care-givers. Some of us never pay attention to our own feelings, only the feelings of others. We are the co-dependents on the planet. We may also be passive-aggressive--individuals who win by losing, because defeating the other person passively was the only defense we had as children.

If, when we are children, our feelings are not accepted as exactly that--just feelings, we learn that our feelings are not acceptable--that they do not please our parents. We begin looking for our parents' reactions rather than looking at how *we* feel about those things. We begin monitoring what we feel and worry that what we do may not be acceptable. We become what Bradshaw calls "human doings" rather than "human beings."

**Pitcher Pete waved off Catcher Cathy's signs, while Batter Bob totally disregarded base Coach Cindy's hit and run signal.
Result: no game today!**

THOSE WHOSE *DOINGS* ARE
EXTERNAL BECOME CO-DEPENDENT

The term "co-dependence" is used frequently in the 1990s. It has numerous definitions. St. John's Hospital in Salina, Kansas published a paper entitled "What is Co-Dependency?" that defines co-dependency as "a set of maladaptive, compulsive behaviors learned by family members in order to

survive in a family which is experiencing great emotional pain and stress...."
The key words here are *in order to survive.* 65

My personal definition of co-dependency used to be "giving to others at one's own expense." In doing research for this book, I adopted a new definition for co-dependency. It is "Acting against our own best interests, without awareness, because we feel it is necessary *to survive.*" Co-dependency is a survival technique. It is a form of bargaining: "You'll love me if I give myself up to you." If the belief that "I am not important" is established early in life, (which is similar to being in a hypnotic trance) co-dependency is the only behavior option available. It is an unconscious response. Whatever the message is, it establishes a core belief--a doctrine from which we act automatically. It is a behavior that meets with our family's approval and that we therefore repeat. It is the only way we know how to be. Any other option is a betrayal of the family system. Behavior on our own behalf is not approved of, and therefore is not considered.

> Liz was the only child of abusive, alcoholic parents. She learned early in life that to survive she had to give herself up (by having no feelings of her own, by becoming passive and compliant, and by taking care of her drunk mother instead of playing with her friends). She got married at 15 in order to escape her abusive home life. Her husband, also an alcoholic, physically and emotionally abused her. When she had a daughter, Liz amazed herself by summoning enough strength to leave him. She raised her daughter until she left to attend college. Later that year Liz met and married Michael. Contrary to what Liz wanted, Michael's parents came to live with them shortly after the marriage. The parents-in-law blamed Liz for any problems they had with Michael, and Liz found herself in the middle of the conflicts. Michael worked late and left his parents' care, and troubles, to Liz.
>
> Michael's father attempted to molest Liz. When Liz confronted Michael, he refuted her report and sided with his father, who denied the allegation. Michael yelled at Liz, called her crazy and blamed her for picking on his parents (just as Liz's mother had blamed her long ago.) Michael slapped her, belittled her, and undermined boundaries she tried to set with her parents-in-law. But the relationship with Michael meant

everything to her, and she could not see beyond it. She felt that she loved Michael, and that the security she felt in being married, took precedence over any manner in which she was treated.

Liz is co-dependent.

Co-dependents have no concept of a self that others can relate to. Whatever small vestige of the self exists is easily given away in order to maintain a relationship. Co-dependents feel literally "like nothing" without the co-dependent relationship. [66]

Co-dependents have no vision of self.

THOSE WHOSE *DOINGS* ARE
INTERNAL BECOME PASSIVE-AGGRESSIVE

Passive-aggressive behavior develops when we cannot maintain emotional equilibrium under circumstances which make we feel helpless, powerless, and ineffective by any direct means. This sense of being out of control and not mattering disturbs our emotional development. A passive-aggressive response is aggressive (although passively expressed) immature behavior, such as pouting, stubbornness, procrastination, inefficiency, or forgetting. It is masochistic because we turn against ourselves. It satisfies us because it gives us a feeling of having some power against an overwhelming powerlessness, the feeling that we are not good-enough, no matter what we do. Passive-aggressive behavior is also a survival technique. The mildest form of passive-aggressiveness is a sort of political stance when we say one thing and mean another. Some statements common in a conversation with a passive-aggressive person are:

"I don't know."

"Nothing, I was just thinking."

"OK, I'll try."

"I'm doing the best I can. What more do you want from me?"

"Oh, sorry, I didn't hear you."

"If I could, I would."

"I'm not angry."

"I'm sorry, it's all my fault. Let's just drop it. What else?"

"I hope I can."

"That sounds good/right. We'll just do it your way."

"I'll be there as soon as I can."

The passive-aggressive defense is developed early in life if we are constantly criticized for our best (that is not good-enough). We learn that we feel better and have more control when we agree with the other person, but then do only what we want to do. By agreeing and appeasing we feel we will not be criticized.

"I hear you, let me have that sink in."

"I'll do it next week, tomorrow...".

"I forgot, I'm sorry, I'll get right to it."

We cannot be held accountable if what we are doing is *still in the works*-- going to be done, being thought about, being tried, or when the "best" is being put forward. The passive-aggressive defense is always successful in defeating the other person. The problem is that when we are passive-aggressive, we are also defeated. We create a *lose-lose position,* but it is one in which the passive-aggressive defense feels safe. The passive-aggressive person allows us to know that "If we both lose, it is better than if you win and I lose." No other option seems available to us. Win-win has not been a part of the passive-aggressive experience.

The devastation caused by passive-aggressiveness results in hostility and anger inside us that never is resolved. The negative feelings remain hidden, unresolved, and never forgotten. Those of us who are involved with a passive-aggressive person feel like we are the crazy ones. The attack that we receive is always subtle. If we offend someone who is passive-aggressive, we can be certain we will be paid back. But we never know exactly *when* it will come or *why* it comes or in *what* form the payback will take. We can be sure, however that the payback *will* come.

"OK defense, let's apply a full court denial attack and fall back into a passive-aggressive zone. Tommy pick up the sarcasm on #42, he is penetrating us badly."

Bob, age 60 wanted a relationship with Robin, age 41. They were friends, and he wanted a more romantic relationship with her. Robin was reluctant to jump into a relationship with Bob because she was not physically "wild about him." He seemed genuine and they had lots of fun together. He was thoughtful and persistent, so she decided to give the relationship a chance. He immediately wanted more physical contact than she did. He thought she was withholding from him and felt helpless to do anything about it. He was angry but did not show it. When she arrived at his apartment after finally agreeing to spend the night, he had not showered, the sheets were dirty, the single beds were separated by a bedside table and there was no food in the house. He denied that there was anything unusual about the condition of the house or himself. He expressed his anger passive-aggressively. He won--by losing. Bob is passive-aggressive.

If what *we do* is all *we are*, then any criticism or hint of criticism is devastating because we feel *completely worthless*. When "human doings" are confronted in any manner, they feel annihilation or loss of love. Therefore, the confrontation is felt as an "attack" and *must* be defended against with great fervor. Those of us who feel unworthy unless everything we do is completely accepted are the most defensive. We cannot maintain emotional equilibrium (our center) under even the minor stress caused by a hint that we are *not right*. After all, we spend our lives making sure that we please others. If we don't, we believe that we *are nothing*. Thus, we have our guard up constantly and are frequently, if not always, defensive.

The following is my hypothesis of how and why defensiveness is so difficult to give up.

THE SENSOR/CENSOR

Freud's original model of the mind is a useful, concrete model for an explanation of the sensor/censor's function. Freud originally postulated that there was a conscious mind (like that of Quadrant I in the *Johari Window*, Figure 5), a preconscious mind, holding material that is near consciousness and might be known through dreams or slips of the tongue that might be located in the hidden or blind quadrants in the *Johari Window*, and an unconscious part of the mind which houses repressed material that is unacceptable to us (found in Quadrant IV in the *Johari Window*.)

A *censor* is an authorized examiner of material, who may prohibit what is considered morally or otherwise objectionable.

A *sensor* is a device, such as a photoelectric cell, that receives and responds to a signal or stimulus, usually for the purpose of sounding an alarm for protection. 67

Between the preconscious and the unconscious is the *sensor/censor*. The *sensor* senses and warns against possible threats to the core belief systems and sounds an alarm in the form of anxiety. The *censor* operates the ego defense mechanisms that prohibit new information from entering conscious awareness that might interfere with existing belief systems and therefore prohibit the possibility of change.

> During the Thanksgiving holiday, Grace, age 52, was planning a 30th birthday party for her daughter, Gayle. Gathering with the same friends in Big Bear during this holiday had been a tradition since Gayle's birth. Grace's first husband had had little to do with his daughter since divorcing Grace 20 years earlier, but he decided to invite Gayle to celebrate his 60th birthday on Thanksgiving. Gayle agreed to forego Grace's planned celebration in order to be with her father. Since Grace had spent her life being co-dependent, her feelings of depressed and mild anger about this was unusual. During a therapy session, she discussed her inability to "shake the depression" or to forget about the birthday party she had planned. She denied that she was angry or disappointed. She said that she wanted Gayle to do whatever she wanted to do for her birthday.
>
> The anger/depression slipped through the *censor* and could not be contained. She couldn't figure our why she was feeling depressed. We discussed how she rarely spoke up for herself. The *sensor* was alerted. She felt uncomfortable and began making "other plans for the party" right during the session. Her *censor* began to protect the deeper belief system: *"I am a bad person when I think about myself. Thinking about myself hurts other people."* Grace decided she had to leave the session early and said she felt better. She repressed the depression and angry feelings and returned to the old belief system. "My feelings don't matter. Pleasing other people is the most important thing." In this instance her *censor* won out.

Grace's depression was a defensive reaction to feeling angry about a thwarted plan to please her daughter for her 30th birthday. In the safety of my office, Grace was able to explore the belief system that *she is a bad person when she thinks about her own wants and feelings.* Grace could admit feeling depressed because it was less threatening than a direct expression of anger. She was able, momentarily, to consider that her anger was a normal, healthy reaction to being disappointed. She was not able to express anger, however, because it was too uncomfortable, because it would be completely contrary to her life-long belief that she was a *compliant, generous person whose needs were not important.* The deeper belief that *thinking about my feelings or my needs hurts others* was activated. The *sensor* alarm went off and the *censor* prohibited any further exploration. A plan to celebrate the birthday in another way emerged. Connecting depression with having needs was too painful for Grace, making her feel like a bad person. Grace had equated having needs with losing love. She no longer felt depressed. The depression itself became repressed. Grace's co-dependence activated the *doing* rather than her *being*!

Joe had been struggling for months to change a friendly relationship to a romantic one. He had been seeing a woman from work for almost a year. Months before, they had had two romantic encounters in which Joe had difficulty maintaining an erection. The woman felt rejected and decided he was not attracted to her "in that way." They were in each other's company constantly, had a great time together, and did not want to see anyone else, but remained "just friends." Joe went along with this arrangement. He enjoyed her and felt he was in love with her. Joe had a rejecting mother and, later, a rejecting step-mother, and as a result felt unlovable. He sabotaged previous relationships in order to avoid being hurt again. His woman friend was from a similar background, except that her rejecting parent was her father.

During one therapy session, Joe discussed confronting her about his desire for their relationship to flourish. He decided to tell her that their friendship could not continue unless they could develop a fuller and more complete relationship. The status-quo was too frustrating for him. He felt confident as he left the office, so in the next session I asked him what happened? He replied, "I didn't say anything. I went out with another girl. It's over. I know she doesn't care about me."

In exploring what happened from the time he left my office until he had dinner with her, he explained he must have misread all her signs of friendship and that he couldn't be vulnerable anymore. He had actually "forgotten" what we had discussed. His *censor* was turned on before he had opened his car door after leaving my office. The window of opportunity was slammed shut when he moved from the safety of my office to the reality of feeling he might be hurt again. His core belief system *I am unlovable. no one will (could) ever love me* was protected by his *censor/sensor* and as a result, his denial and rationalization defense mechanisms took over.

WHEN THE *CENSOR* DOESN'T ALLOW US TO LET GO OF "OLD" STUFF

How can we be so determined or so near to awareness of what we need to do and then *not do it????* *What a puzzle!* I believe this phenomenon happens any time we want to break a habit or change in any form. It is the reason that New Year's resolutions rarely work, why going on a diet and sticking to a diet is so difficult, and why the promise, "I'll never do that again" is usually broken. It is why self-help books rarely help!

Why does giving up something for Lent, Passover or Ram A Dan usually work?

Many Christian denominations observe the 40-day Lenten season between Ash Wednesday and Easter. One of the practices is to give something up for Lent, such as candy, alcohol, sleeping in on weekends, going to movies, and so on in order to recall the sacrifice that Jesus Christ made. This 40-day "change" in behavior is usually successful because the belief system regarding this religious practice is greater than the belief system we have for doing whatever it was we chose to give up. In the Jewish religion, the practice of eating only unleavened bread during Passover to reminds Jewish people of their deliverance from slavery and the hasty exodus from Egypt. In the Islamic religion, during the month of Ram A Dan, no food or drink is consumed between sunrise and sunset.

These religious customs illustrate how we can get beyond our core beliefs when we give up a habit or treasured behavior for a purpose greater than ourselves. The Twelve-Step movement of Alcoholic Anonymous is somewhat based on this concept as well.

As the self-in-process explores the ego defense mechanisms, associations that are less unacceptable are allowed to pass the *sensor*, allowing for access to reasons for the defenses in the first place.

Even the act of recognizing that we *are defensive* is a major breakthrough.

Another major breakthrough is when we begin recognizing patterns in our lives such as getting fired repeatedly from our job, marrying an abusive man for the second (or third) time, having relationships with unavailable people who cannot commit to us, finding mates who are unproductive or completely dependent upon us, and so on. Patterns repeated in our lives may indicate what we have not yet resolved. We may be blind to patterns, or we may see them and try to hide them. We may not be aware of these patterns until they are pointed out to us. One day we "wake up" and see them and ask "Why?" The "why" can slip by the *sensor* because it *is a pattern*.

Patterns are a way of manifesting what is blind to our consciousness. When we begin to face these patterns, we may begin to feel uncomfortable, and anxiety may arise. The anxiety sounds an alarm for the defense system to mobilize so that additional or worse issues are not released.

Repressed material is repressed because what happened in the past was overwhelmingly devastating. When we get close to these memories, the painful feelings return and we close down all over again.

> Rita, the 14-year-old girl at San Gabriel High School, needed to repress the memory of her father's death because that memory made her feel that she had murdered him by her thoughts.

The problem is that our initial associations or "insights" are based on thoughts and memories in the pre-conscious. That is, the safer information that has passed through the *sensor* as acceptable. It is not a deeper, repressed idea that is kept in the unconscious by the *censor*. At this point we must keep in mind why the defenses were employed in the first place.

> "The tenacity with which children attempt throughout their lives to deal

141

with their need to feel loved by the parents may indicate that they are convinced that their lives depend on it, and this suggests a link with their fear of annihilation....It therefore suggests that far deeper concerns than the pleasure principle dominate the child's psychic processes. Rather than instinctual gratification, the child's major preoccupation appears to be survival. This latter seems to rest on two related elements, fear of annihilation at the hands of the parents, and the need to feel loved by them." [68]

When we acquire new insights, and become more aware, our trust and good feelings about change and growth must override the pain and fear we have experienced in the past. New opportunities for growth will remain out of consciousness as long as our ego feels that the new awareness will be hurtful and dangerous. We associate *not saying our feelings* with not hurting our parents or not being belittled or hurt ourselves. This association is like a stimulus-response. We do not say how we feel. We feel good (calm and not anxious) because we have not hurt someone important to us, or we feel good (safe and not attacked) because we have escaped what is perceived as an attack. The association between not saying how we feel and the fact that our feelings were never encouraged *is an insight*. This connection between cause and effect can be made in the conscious mind because this piece of data from the unconscious has *slipped by* the *sensor/censor*. But the extent of a person's belief system is much deeper and far more insidious.

Some belief systems are not ours but were swallowed whole from things we heard from our parents. In my family, some of these beliefs were, "Early to bed and early to rise makes a man healthy, wealthy and wise." Another was, "Waste not, want not."

The latter of the family beliefs came back in its negative sense one evening when my husband served a salad he had made for dinner. We were relaxing and enjoying eating together when I looked at the large salad and thought there would certainly be salad left over. "You made too much salad," I said. We were both surprised by my critique. I thoroughly enjoy left-overs and often plan a larger meal in the evening so that I can

142

have enough for lunch the next day. Where did that remark come from? "You made too much" had slipped by my *sensor* to reveal a message of "waste not" from my unconscious. We both laughed (rewarding the insight), and I realized that I no longer needed that particular warning in my life.

The deeper, more insidious belief system might be that "to be loved, I must not waste food."

When Howard, the man who couldn't be angry at his alcoholic father, married an alcoholic woman whom he wanted to *fix*, he was punished when he expressed his feelings. One of the feelings which may have emerged but was never expressed was "I hate my father for never paying attention to me." If hating his father made Howard a bad person (creating a limiting belief system), then his deeper belief system was activated when, as an adult, he realized that not stating his feelings was a result of a belief put together when he was a child.

Warren, remained the "tough guy" instead of dealing with his inability to have an intimate relationship. The parishioners (of the church whose pastor molested the children) put up altar rails and locked doors instead of dealing with their rage at being betrayed by their pastor. Jack ended his relationship rather than experience the anxiety of attempting a more intimate (sexual) involvement. Janet, the school teacher, reconnected with her parents instead of developing a relationship of her own, in order to protect her belief that her father would die if she had a relationship of her own.

When, as adults we encounter a belief from our past, we "panic" and revert back to protecting our attacker. "But my dad worked so hard for us" might have been Howard's defense. His reward was the insight of connection. His punishment was the anxiety of the limiting belief system. Studies show that human beings will do much more to avoid pain than to gain pleasure. Change, therefore, does not just happen.

REINFORCING CONSCIOUSNESS

If the awareness can be tolerated and new behavior based on that awareness can be risked, then awareness alone can serve as a reinforcer for more repressed material to reach consciousness. Only then can we risk more new behavior, based on this awareness. Awareness alone, however, does not equal awareness plus new behavior. The key is allowing what has been repressed for survival to be accessed and tolerated so that we can examine it in the present.

Remember, our defense mechanisms were formed to protect us from the trauma of surviving in an un-empathetic world--a world that did not understand how we felt or who we were.

A self-in-process is needed to transcend the defensive ego. The relationship between the *self-in-process* and the *wounded child* (the ego) must be healed before we can release the old defense mechanisms. We need resolution of past issues. It is actually the continuity of the self-in-process, functioning apart from our attachments, that allows us to let go of that which is no longer a threat.

Before proceeding to the discussion of resolution and separation, I want to discuss two of the most destructive barriers to the possibility of change--defensiveness and procrastination. These characteristics are strong elements in co-dependent, and passive-aggressive personalities and are the *censor/sensor's* "best friends."

DEFENSIVENESS
THE #1
KILLER OF CHANGE

"The problem in defense is how far you can go without
destroying from within what you're trying to defend from without."
—Dwight D. Eisenhower

Defensiveness stops change and growth! When we are defensive we catapult ourselves into unreality. Our ego defense mechanisms protect what we feel will threaten, hurt, or destroy us. To tolerate life, we block or alter reality to feel secure. We fool ourselves.

Once we become *defensive, all communication stops*. Further discussion is a waste of time. The strongest *barrier to change* is defensiveness. Defensiveness protects what we fear is a "fragile ego", but which interferes with an ego functioning at a level that could easily handle the situation.

When we are not validated by our mothers, we do not develop freely. Our fragile egos and undeveloped selves feel that any criticism will cause a devastating crack in our being. When Bradshaw describes the vulnerability of the child's ego, he notes that the more vulnerable the ego is, the less criticism it can tolerate.

We develop strategies to avoid the hurt of being criticized. We may verbally "blow up," criticize, bring up faults of our critic, become sarcastic, or not respond at all. We might to choose to be passive and turn red, cry, pout, or run out of the room. We might build up resentment and "get" the critic later. We might ignore our critic and pretend we didn't hear what was said. In order to avoid conflict, we might hurriedly agree with everything the critic says.

When we hold in our anger and hurt, we run the risk of developing physical symptoms such as headaches, gastritis, ulcers, and spastic colitis. When we sit on our feelings and don't express them, we get depressed. [69]

"Isn't that cute? Johnny's building up resentment."

THE OPPOSITE OF DEFENSIVENESS

A confident, centered person (a self-in-process) desires connectedness, relatedness, and clear communication to enhance connection and relationships. The self-in-process expects the best in people and expects positive interactions. When a comment or action is perceived by the self-in-process as negative, the self-in-process is *surprised*. A self-in-process wants more information to re-establish the connectedness and clearly understand the problem.

If clarification results in a deliberate, vicious attack or punishment, then setting a boundary is necessary. This boundary says,

> *"I am not available for attack."* Or

> *"I am not available to someone who hurts me or is toxic to me."*

A self-in-process feels comfortable feeling and saying,

> *"I will remove myself from any situation in which my boundaries are not respected."*

"Honey, your words are so delicious.
Please tell me more about you and your day!"

THE CONCEPT OF DEFENSELESSNESS

One of my friends is a very defensive person, quick to "protect himself" from the slightest hint of criticism. He perceives criticism when he is clearly not being criticized and, he anticipates criticism when none is forthcoming. I asked him to listen to an audio tape of Deepak Chopra discussing "defensiveness." Dr. Chopra says,

> "Rationalizations are just excuses for the things that happen to us. It is a change of perception that is necessary...". Most people spend their entire life defending that they are correct. So the moment you stop trying to do that you are approaching defenselessness. Defenselessness is actually the key to invincibility. When you let down all your defenses, there is nothing to attack. I'm reminded of a statement Mikhail Gorbachev made a few years ago to President Reagan. He said, "We're going to do something terrible to you, we are going to deprive you of an enemy". When you let down all your defenses nobody can attack you because there is nothing to attack. That, really, is ultimate power. Ultimate power does not allow the birth of an enemy and the mechanics of that is simple, effective defenselessness. 70

After hearing this, my friend said, "I won't be defensive anymore. I will be dominated and gouged." He was as surprised as I was to hear this statement. Dr. Chopra said something he was ready to hear. As a result his belief system "snuck out" past his *sensor/censor*.

DEFENSELESSNESS?

The idea of not having defenses may seem horrifying. Yet, putting up a defense takes energy. Building walls, hauling out the artillery, installing monitoring devices, maintaining constant watchfulness is exhausting. If it is necessary, it is worth it. If it is not necessary, it is a waste of time, energy, and focus.

Imagine living in a quiet neighborhood with considerate, thoughtful neighbors in a safe community where the crime rate is the lowest in the country. Putting up barricades, digging moats, and installing gun stations manned by hired marksmen around the our yard would probably not elicit kudos from our neighbors. They would fear that the guns might go off. Most likely, our efforts to be safe and secure would cause more trouble than they would prevent.

On the other hand, if my energy was spent getting to know my neighbors by inviting them in my home, had a party, perhaps even gave one a key in case I locked myself out or needed them to water the plants while I was on vacation, I might appear defenseless. But in fact, I would be stronger because of the openness and trust we would have for each other.

> My parents have lived in the same house and neighborhood for more than 50 years. About 20 years ago, the quality of the neighborhood seemed to decline and the crime rate went up. A TV was stolen out of one neighbor's living room while he was weeding in the back yard. My mother found a young man in the basement and yelled at him to "Get out," and he did. The neighbors decided to fight this problem together and formed one of the first Neighborhood Watches in our city. To accomplish this, all the neighbors attended a weekly meeting so they could get acquainted and know who belonged on the block. If a stranger appeared on the street, the person was courteously approached and asked the nature of his or her business. The neighbors started Christmas caroling together, and held block parties on Halloween. The crime stopped completely. The neighborhood was defenseless in the sense that doors were left unlocked--as before, the police were not summoned or needed, and guns were not purchased. By getting to know each other, the neighbors formed a block-sized community that became invincible.

If we fear becoming defenseless, it is because we were not given a basic sense of trust when we were very young. We are locked into mistrust (See Table 1) and feel we have no choice. We long for belonging and unity with someone, but we never seem to find it. We become preoccupied with pain and expect failure. We are most likely to rely on medication like anti-depressants, anti-anxiety agents, alcohol, nicotine or caffeine to survive. We feel being "ourselves" does not warrant the attention and approval we long for. We *defend ourselves* constantly because *we do not feel we are OK*. We are extra-sensitive to any type of criticism. If our already small amount of esteem is shattered, we fear there will be nothing left in us (See Table 1.)

HEALTHY COMMUNICATION

The short list below describes the steps to healthy communication.

1. Listen carefully to what is being said.

2. Figure out how we feel about what is being said.

3. State what we feel about what was said.

4. State what we need from the other person.

If we feel attacked or criticized, the healthy (not defensive) responses to Step #3 would be:

"I feel attacked"

"That feels terrible. Could you clarify what you mean?"

"You sound angry. Please say more. I'm not sure I understand."

"I'm feeling criticized."

"Ouch, that hurts!"

Another healthy response is to listen actively. Tom Gordon, in his book, *Parent Effectiveness Training*, thoroughly discusses active listening. [71] He makes it clear that we cannot "active listen" when we feel attacked or are emotionally involved in situation. The goal is to discover if the *perceived attack* is real or imagined. If it's imagined or assumed, we are defending nothing. If it is real, there will be plenty of time to call out the militia.

ACTIVE LISTENER

Certainly, criticism is an attack of sorts. We all feel hurt when we are criticized. But we are not helping ourselves if we react defensively. Active listening is a technique in which we attempt to let the other person know that we have heard what they said. When we active listen we use non-defensive phrases like,

"Are you saying..."

"I hear that you want..."

"Let me understand, you feel that...," and so on.

These kinds of responses are positive ways of making sure that we know what it is we heard before we react. Active listening allows us to separate someone else's perceptions from our own reality.

Stephen Covey in his *Applications of the Seven Habits of Highly Effective People,* states that one primary rule of good communication is to restate what the other person has said before we make our own point. 72

ASSERTIVENESS

Once we *clearly hear* what is being said, we need to identify how we feel about it and state our feelings to the speaker.

Our feelings might range from sorrow to anger. If what is said makes us feel sad, then perhaps we need an apology. If we feel angry, we may need to work out some sort of resolution. To receive an apology or resolve a misunderstanding we must speak our feelings and needs, assertively.

Most of us have difficulty being assertive because we are terrified about the results.

> *If we express our needs and wants, will we be criticized or rejected?*

This response is a result of being told, as children, that we were "bad" because of how we felt. Each time we did something that did not make our parents happy, we felt judged, wrong, or bad. In time, we learned to feel "bad" *each time* we were criticized. We never learned to use criticism positively as a means to grow or as a means to distinguish between destructive and constructive comments.

If we could treat each statement given to us as if it were a piece of food. Once we take it in and chew it, we have the option to spit it out or swallow it, in part or in totality. To shut our lips is to cut off the possibility of that piece of food nourishing us and being a part of our growth.

If we feel criticized and react, we prohibit growth. What is even more debilitating is that the possibility of challenging or changing any existing belief system is also prohibited.

On the other hand, if we can heal our vulnerable inner child, listen to what

153

is said to us and respond rather than react, then we have a golden opportunity to explore, understand, and change. We can choose to be aware and choose to act on that awareness.

When we defend ourselves for the sake of feeling safe, we lose. If we listen and respond non-defensively, we win.

THE DIFFERENCE BETWEEN DEFENSIVENESS AND SETTING BOUNDARIES

"It is not difficult to attain enlightenment,
but it is difficult to keep
a beginner's mind."
—Suski Roche

We have been discussing ego defense mechanisms which are unconsciously acquired, involuntary dynamics that protect us from shame, anxiety, or loss of self-esteem. We then discussed defensiveness as the number one killer of change.

We are defensive when we feel attacked or perceive that there might be danger and we feel we need to protect ourselves. The unconscious defensive reaction is not the most effective means of accomplishing this protection.

The healthier, conscious means of protecting ourselves against a *here and now perceived attack* is boundary setting.

A *boundary* is the extent beyond which an activity or function cannot or should not take place. 73 Healthy boundary setting is a conscious process that a self-in-process can employ in order to stay centered and balanced in communication and relationships.

UNHEALTHY BOUNDARIES

Charles Whitfield describes signs of *UNHEALTHY* boundaries as

☐ Telling all.

☐ Talking at an intimate level at the first meeting.

☐ Falling in love with a new acquaintance.

☐ Falling in love with anyone who reaches out.

☐ Being overwhelmed or preoccupied with a person.

☐ Acting on the first sexual impulse.

☐ Being sexual for our partner, not ourself.

☐ Going against personal values or rights to please others.

☐ Not noticing when someone else displays inappropriate boundaries.

☐ Accepting food, gifts, touch, or sex that we don't want.

156

☐ Touching a person without asking.

☐ Taking as much as we can get for the sake of getting.

☐ Allowing someone to take as much as they can from us.

☐ Letting others direct our life.

☐ Letting others describe our reality.

☐ Believing others can anticipate our needs.

☐ Expecting others to fill our needs automatically.

☐ Falling apart so someone will take care of us.

☐ Abusing oneself.

☐ Putting up with sexual or physical abuse.

☐ Abusing food or substances.

Dr. Whitfield also assures us that it is never our responsibility to

☐ Give what we really don't want to give.

☐ Sacrifice our integrity to anyone.

☐ Do more than we have time to do.

☐ Drain our strength for others.

- ☐ Listen to unwise council.

- ☐ Retain an unfair relationship.

- ☐ Be anyone but exactly who we are.

- ☐ Conform to unreasonable demands.

- ☐ Follow the crowd.

- ☐ Be 100% perfect.

- ☐ Put up with unpleasant situations.

- ☐ Please unpleasant people.

- ☐ Bear the burden of another's misbehavior.

- ☐ Do something we really cannot do.

- ☐ Love unlovable people.

- ☐ Endure our own negative thoughts.

- ☐ Feel guilty toward our inner desires.

- ☐ Submit to overbearing conditions.

- ☐ Apologize for being ourselves.

- ☐ Meekly let life pass us by. 74

In fact, it *is our responsibility* not to let *any* of the situations happen.

Instead, we can set clear, direct limits so that we do not find ourselves in these predicaments. Being defensive in the face of aggressions only postpones the work that needs to be done. Clear boundary setting increases communication and stops behavior that is toxic to our growth. If we set a boundaries when we feel we are closing down (withdrawing), then we do not have to be defensive. We can say,

"That's all I can hear right now. Please stop. We can talk later."

We do not have to use defenses that distort reality and stop communication in order to regain our center.

REACTING TO ATTACKS

Human beings, and animals have an automatic response to feeling attacked. We immediately protect ourselves by putting up a defense. This defense is automatic.

Our cat, Minny, will hiss if she thinks we are going to hurt her. An innocent, unintentional gesture that seems threatening to her elicits a hiss. But, as soon as she knows that we do not intend to harm her, she immediately relaxes and purrs.

If indeed we are being attacked, we need to know how to defend ourselves. If, however, we are not being attacked, our *defensiveness destroys any possibility of intimacy and communication.*

Fear of intimacy and commitment comes from the belief system that getting close will be painful. Fear of intimacy may mean a fear of being smothered, needing to fulfill someone else's expectations, being a victim of betrayal (incest), being abused (physical or emotional abuse from parents), or being required to keep secrets (being sucked into something we cannot reveal and therefore become responsible for). We do not need to defend against these fears. We have a right to set boundaries stating that we are not available to participate in being victimized, being abused, or in keeping secrets.

Usually we do not recognize our own defensiveness, and when it is pointed out we feel angry and respond defensively. We may snap back, "I'm not being defensive!" or "I'm not yelling, I'm just being emphatic!" The use of defense mechanisms is a sincere attempt to set boundaries and survive the perceived attack. The perception has to do with the belief system underlying it. Defenses and defensiveness are not healthy boundaries but are, in fact, the opposite.

Defensiveness is a sure-fire way to elicit further attack, because when we cut off communication by our defensiveness, our perceived "attacker" feels helpless. The feeling of helplessness promotes a sense of violence. In order to break down the barriers, the perceived attacker talks more loudly, feels more angry and becomes more irrational because he or she has been cut off. This expression of frustration and helplessness is futile. The *only way* to deal with a defensive person is *not to* persist when defensiveness comes up.

When we talk to someone who becomes defensive, we might say:

"You seem defensive, do you feel I am attacking you?"

"I feel misunderstood. It is not my intention to make you feel criticized."

Or, simply stop and wait for a more opportune time to continue the discussion.

We might as well stop, because as soon as someone becomes *defensive*, the *conversation is virtually over.*

A couple was separated, contemplating divorce. The marriage counseling was a "last-ditch" effort to see if the relationship could work.

One problem was that Mitzie had some preconceived ideas about how she should be treated if she was to feel loved. Her husband, Lee did not know to do these things. Mitzie looked forward to going places, and Lee was a last minute planner. Mitzie wanted Lee to come home immediately

160

after work, to spend time with her. Lee wanted to spend an hour or two with friends after work. When Lee called home to ask if it was OK to "have a beer," Mitzie would say "Yes", but by the time Lee came home, she felt unloved. Lee felt that whatever he did, it was not good-enough and that he could never do enough to please her. The more Mitzie demanded of Lee, the more he withdrew.

In counseling, Mitzi began listing the things she wanted in order to feel loved. One was that Lee to call her from work every day. Lee felt that, on some days, he would be out of the office or too busy. When he agreed to call four to five times per week. Mitzie looked crushed and said, "You call the kids every day--maybe even several times a day." Lee got defensive, "I don't call them all the time or every day. I call them when I can, because I miss them."

I intervened, pointing out his defensiveness. When he examined his feelings instead, he could get in touch with what he was feeling. He said that he felt pushed. He wanted to feel he could call because he wanted to call, not because he had to call. Mitzie wanted him to want to call every day or she felt rejected. Lee set a boundary:

"Mitzie, he said, you have to let me be me. If that isn't enough for you, let's find out. Maybe I'll want to call you more than once a day, but let's both try it our this way. Let me promise you I will never go without calling you at least every other day. You can call me anytime you feel you want to talk to me. If you call me at work and I am brief, it will be because I am with someone, or very busy, but not because I don't want to talk to you. OK?"

THE HEALTHY ALTERNATIVE

The clear boundary set by Lee allowed Mitzie to relax and created a way for the relationship to begin again. When clear boundaries are set, intimacy is encouraged and commitment is a possibility. Lee's defensiveness was non-specific. He was grasping at anything in order not to feel attacked. Before counseling, he felt like he was fighting his way out of a bag because the enemy was everywhere! Boundaries provide ways to say

> *"This part of our relationship is not OK."*

Agreeing on boundaries opens the door for trust, respect, and further communication.

Defenses are constructed to protect a fragile ego. Boundaries are set to enhance the self-in-process and increase healthy interaction.

Awareness of our "defensiveness" allows us to weather the feelings of "being attacked." If we can say,

> *"I am feeling defensive"* or

> *"I'm feeling attacked"*

rather than *being* defensive, then we can remain centered, and we can let the other person know that communication has stopped until we *feel safe* again.

Unfortunately, awareness can produce a new killer of change--a demon called *procrastination,* which is the topic of the next chapter.

PROCRASTINATION THE #2 KILLER OF CHANGE

"Only those who dare to go too far
can possibly find out how far one can go."
—T.S. Eliot

The Procrastinator's Code

I must be perfect
Everything I do should go easily and without effort.
It's safer to do nothing than to take a risk and fail.
I should have no limitations.
If it's not done right, it's not worth doing at all.
I must avoid being challenged.
If I succeed, someone will get hurt.
If I do well this time, I must always do well.
Following someone else's rules means I'm giving in and I'm not in control.
I can't afford to let go of anything or anyone.
If I expose my real self, people won't like me.
There is a right answer, and I'll wait until I find it.
—Jane B. Burka and Lenora Yuen

With the main field off, the
procrastinators become keen and
edgy approaching the blocks

Jud was driving his truck, when he was broadsided when a woman driving a Cadillac ran a stop sign. It was obvious that the woman was at fault. Jud delayed calling his own insurance company because he was waiting for a copy of the police report so that he could prove the accident was not his fault. When he received the report he was so relieved that he again waited to call his insurance company fearing that they would get mad at him and make him feel bad again.

In the meantime, the woman's insurance company settled the claim, sent him a check for $3,000, and told him that since they had not heard from his insurance company, $3,000 this was all they could pay. Jud is stuck. His truck is inoperable, and he doesn't have enough money to buy a new vehicle--even though he is insured. He won't get help from the insurance company because he's afraid his rate will increase as a result of the accident.

Jud is a victim of his own procrastination.

Procrastination is defined as the process of deferring action, to delay; to put off till another day or time. It is also defined as the process of putting off intentionally and habitually and for a reason deemed to be reprehensible such as laziness or indifference to responsibility. [75] The opposite of procrastination is risk. Procrastination is characterized by the 4 S's: Safe, secure, scared and sad.

When postponing activities causes consequences that harm us internally (making us feel bad about ourselves) or externally (causing us to lose opportunities or jeopardize relationships), then the procrastination hinders or stops growth. Procrastination is debilitating and is nearly as devastating as defensiveness.

In some cases postponing does not have negative consequences. We may run out of time to accomplish all we may want to do. Or, perhaps we are a "low-key" personality. If so, some to do's on your lists may have to get done in their "own sweet time." This is not the kind of procrastination discussed here.

> I procrastinate about doing things I hate doing. The thought of filling out forms of any kind bothers me. I put them first on my "to do" list. Still I can think of a million things to do with the time set aside for dealing with them. It is also difficult for me to write a report, a dissertation, a letter, and this book. When it's time to write something, cleaning my "messy drawers" takes precedence. I feel a powerful urge to "clean out just one drawer," this file, or to re-arrange items on a shelf.

Norman throws out defensively a "procrastination" pitch.

I worry that I have nothing to say, and what I do say will be stupid. If I continue to postpone and procrastinate, then I will not grow or improve my writing skills. Awareness that I am procrastinating allows me to clean just one drawer--or not! I can joke about this behavior with my husband by saying, "I'm going to do some writing today. I wonder which drawer needs cleaning out." We laugh, and I know I have some choices about how to prioritize my day.

There are three major reasons for procrastinating: Maintaining control, fear of failure and fear of success.

MAINTAINING CONTROL

Jack is a long-term client who was raised by a unavailable mother and an absent father. He was born 14 years after his next older sibling. Neither parent ever hugged him, and they only touched him when absolutely necessary. He grew up feeling unlovable and unacceptable, having only one friend in all his young years. In college, he had a nervous breakdown, and he lived the next 30 years with his mother. He was 49-years-old when she died, and as an adult he had never had a relationship with anyone, not even with a male buddy.

When he began psychotherapy, he started to explore the dynamics of his life. He had great insights about what an unusual life he had chosen to lead, and why. He marveled at how he had survived, but he would not take any action to change his social situation. He knew what he had to do, but he procrastinated about taking any action.

Jack would read and take into himself the noble characters he read about. When I talked him into placing an ad (it took him over a year to actually place the ad) to meet someone in the local single's newspaper he described himself as having the attributes of the characters he read about. He listed interests of the fictional characters as his own (a denial of his own limitations) including athletics, theater and opera.

In reality, he had never worked out athletically--even walking to the bus tired him. He had never attended the theater or heard an opera. The difference between Jack's description of himself in the ad and Jack in person shocked the women who answered his ad. He met with rejection and thus validated his childhood feelings (the unresolved issue) he had with his parents that he was not a lovable person.

When he became more "real," his ad read: "Scared to death. If you feel the same, call..." He was deluged with calls and has begun having a series of first dates and finally has a female friend.

Jack obviously lacks experience. He is unaware of normal social amenities. When I suggested that he call and thank the woman after a date, he heard what I said, but decided that the call represented too much of a commitment. He wasn't sure he wanted to "be stuck with them forever" (a sign of commitment phobia). He waited a week or more before contacting women he dated. And sometimes, he never called back. In therapy sessions, Jack informed me that he would *feel weak* if he followed my directions. Jack felt that if he called women in his own time, he would remain *in control* and not lose sight of what he wanted to do. The bottom line was that he procrastinated to the point of *emotional paralysis* more often than not.

The issue of control is central in persons who feel that the only way to cope with the world is to make sure they never lose control. This type of control, however, is *passive-aggressive* because there is no action, only delay.

> Marty joined one of my groups. During his fourth meeting, he looked as if he were going to explode. His face was red and he had a sour, angry look on his face. Nancy, a group member, expressed her preference for his previous behavior which had been expressive and open. Marty admitted he was withholding his feelings. I asked him how it felt to withhold. He described what I believe is the reward of passive-aggressive behavior. He said, "I feel warm and comforted. It feels safe and I don't feel vulnerable, I feel in control."

FEAR OF FAILURE

The *fear of failure* is fear of not meeting someone else's expectations, of not being able to measure up. It is also fear of not meeting our *own* expectations. Perfectionists and those of us who have been criticized severely in childhood feel that:

What we do won't be good-enough anyway.

168

Testing our *real* ability is too threatening. We can passively tell ourselves that we could have done better, *if we just had more time.*

This fear of rejection makes us postpone doing the task. We rationalize about not doing it.

"I don't have all the material to begin."

"I'll feel in a better mood to begin tomorrow."

"I don't have time."

"This (other thing) has to be done now."

It may be a reality that what is expected of us is too much, and beginning the task will inevitably meet with failure. Procrastination here is *in place of setting* a realistic boundary and/or declining to do the task in the first place. Putting-off doing something we should not have accepted in the first place will not solve the problem.

> Robert was a good runner and won some medals at school. His father, however, bragged about Robert being a great track and field star, and Olympic hopeful. Robert put-off filling out the application to attend camp for Olympic hopefuls until it was too late. In his heart, Robert knew (or thought he knew) that he wasn't *that* good.

FEAR OF SUCCESS

A young teen may not do her assignment or do it at the last minute, essentially "faking being stupid." She may relate failure with peer acceptance and success with rejection.

The phrase, "fear of success," does sound puzzling to many of us. Why would anyone feel afraid of success? Success is feared because we fear what

169

will be expected of us or that we will be punished for success. If we fear commitment and we succeed, then we feel we are committed to the highest level of our achievement.

Fear of success hooks into another one

Another reason for the fear of success is the belief in the myth that the "bigger they are, the harder they fall." We feel that life has to have a balance, and that if we achieve greatness then it will be balanced by a tragedy. Think of the people who have succeeded where others have not--Abraham Lincoln, Martin Luther King, Jr., John Fitzgerald Kennedy, Robert Kennedy, Donald Trump, Richard Nixon, Michael Jackson, Gandhi, O.J. Simpson. We can point to the tragedy in each of their lives and give ourselves an excuse *to wait and see*. We can say, "Look at what happens to these people who seem to have it all."

Other reasons we might fear success may be more unconscious. We may have seen one or both of our parents pay a high price for financial success and not want to live our lives that way. If our self-image does not match our accomplishments, we might sabotage our potential success.

> In the tennis world I have heard detailed accounts of underdogs (persons with a lower tennis rating) who often almost win a match against the player who is the top-dog (rated higher in ability and picked to win by a tournament committee.)

Fear of change is actually the fear of success and a major cause of procrastination.

Some of us fear that, if we are successful, we will betray our parents, siblings or spouse. We worry that others in our lives will be unable to handle our success. Those people would feel bad, so we make an effort to maintain the success hierarchy as it is. Persons with chemical dependency have belief systems that hinder them from giving up their dependency. (See Chapter 1)

The examples in this chapter reveal a particular core belief system. Jack's sensitivity to my suggestions that he follow-up with the women he dated meant he was a wimp. Robert believed that he would displease his father (and lose his love) if the risks he took did not measure up. My need to clean out drawers, instead of writing this book, shows my fear that it will not meet the expectations of clients and friends who read it (or perhaps, that I will.)

In the classic movie *Harold and Maude,* Harold told Maude that he realized that he enjoyed being dead. Maude replied,

"Oh, Harold, lots of people enjoy being dead but they aren't dead really. They are just backing away from life. Reach out, take a chance, get hurt even, play as well as you can. Go team, go. Give me an L, give me an I, give me a V, give me an E. L-I-V-E. Live! Otherwise, you have nothing to talk about in the locker room."

Amen.

CHAPTER 15

THE PRICE OF UNAWARENESS

"False beliefs are your worst enemy after unawareness."
—M. Scott Peck

"You will find evidence to support your conclusions."
—Stephen Covey

Given the importance of belief systems and how much they direct and control our lives, it is shocking how few people learn what their belief systems are. It may be less remarkable to know that the people most dissatisfied with their lives, are who are the least self-aware, and who most lack a solid sense of identity. 77 There are reasons for this lack of awareness.

The more dysfunctional our family is, the more unaware the family members remain, because awareness is a challenge to the family myth "that everything is OK." Awareness is perceived as betrayal. Being "happy" or successful can also be perceived as a betrayal.

DYSFUNCTIONAL FAMILY ACTIVITIES

Dr. Whitfield lists the behaviors and characteristics commonly found in dysfunctional families. These are also the characteristics that remain outside the family's awareness.

☐ Lack of respect and empathy

☐ Neglect or mistreatment

☐ Criticism and blaming

☐ Lack of humor

☐ Intrusiveness

☐ Conditional love

☐ Superficiality: Issues that cannot or will not be resolved

☐ Feelings not respected

☐ No sense of belonging

☐ Constant yelling or conflict

☐ Individuality discouraged or punished

☐ Scarcity principle vs principle of abundance

☐ Role reversals (child assuming inappropriate age or task functions)

☐ No acknowledgement of feelings [78]

If our family is dysfunctional we are not getting the amount of validation we must have to see ourselves OK in the world. If we do not receive validation at the age appropriate time, then we continues to seek acknowledgement and approval, which may keep us dependent for a life-time. We need to keep in mind that the more we are abused, the less awareness we will have as an adult. *Less awareness leaves us with fewer choices.*

Co-dependency and passive-aggressiveness are behaviors typical of us whose parents did not validate, empathize or mirror us. For us to change these behaviors we must learn to resolve the issues that face us today.

As adults, what was done to us as children we continue to do to ourselves. If we were ignored as children, we ignore ourselves as adults. If we were abused as children, we abuse ourselves as adults by how we allow others to treat us, or how we treat ourselves. If we were expected to prove our worth by *doing,* we continue to prove our worth by *doing more.* If we had to get sick to get attention, then we continue to get sick when we need attention.

Child Validation Day

Unconscious beliefs, that is, beliefs that are acted out without awareness, imprison us and confine us to a limited version of our lives. Throughout our lives we continue to be limited by these false beliefs. When reality is dangerous, painful, or incongruous with these beliefs, the false beliefs become more deeply rooted.

> My own belief systems about working come from my dad. He taught me that: "You can't get something for nothing," and "You can have whatever you want, but you must work to get it." Although this belief has motivated me through many years, it also has caused me discomfort and dis-ease. As a result of this belief system, I work very hard--harder than is necessary.
>
> When I used to think about working less, or taking a vacation, I felt uncomfortable, anxious, and worried. I asked myself, "Who will provide for me if I don't work? How will I be able to maintain my lifestyle?
>
> When I worked for the school systems, I never missed a day of work, but I was sick most of my time off! These feelings had nothing to do with reality, my husband's income, or the actual amount of money in the bank. These feelings were based on data programmed into my unconscious during my formative years.

In my therapy groups, I usually begin the session by asking each member to state his/her goals for that session. Sometimes my request is to describe what he/she would rather *not* bring up in this session. It is always amazing to me to hear each response:

> *"I don't want to talk about my dad."*

> *"I don't want to talk about my marijuana use."*

> *"I don't want to talk about my feelings about Susie"*
> *(another member).*

> *"I don't want to show how angry I am."*

176

All the "I don't wants" cause anxiety. Anxiety in the cases above come from issues that are unresolved.

With further exploration, group members added their reasons (beliefs).

"If I talk about my dad, I know I'll be angry at him and that means I'm a bad son." (Instead, "I will devote my life trying to change my wife, who, incidentally, is just like my dad.")

"If I talk about my marijuana use, you'll know why I'm not getting on with my life and why I continue hiding out in my house alone." (Instead, "I will devote my life to feeling alone and sorry for myself, which incidentally is exactly how my mother lives her life.")

"If I tell you about my feelings about Susie, it might reveal something about me that you might not like me. If I say how angry I am feeling, you'll hate me for not being nice. I will make you unhappy because of how I feel, so I pretend not to feel. I am a reserved person. This belief system allows me not to realize that I am withholding from you rather than being reserved." (Instead, "I will not have to experience any anxiety and continue to live a so-so existence just as my father did.")

DOES WHAT WE ARE DOING REALLY MAKE SENSE?

It is important to examine *what* we are doing in light of *why* we are doing it. Ask, "Does the reason I am not doing this *really make sense?*"

Several years ago it appeared that veteran tennis champions John McEnroe and Jimmy Connors would retire from tennis. Connors offered to coach McEnroe if he would return to the game. John laughed and said he wasn't coming back. Shortly after that, Connors "got back into tennis" himself and gave the world one of the most exciting U.S. Open tournaments ever played. He rejected the belief system that he was too old. After Connors' brilliant showing at the U.S. Open, John McEnroe also made his comeback.

In Shirley MacLaine's book *Dance While You Can,* she relates a conversation she had with her mother. Shirley invited her mother to come to California and her mother asked if Shirley could afford the plane tickets. Shirley assured her she could; then Shirley wrote:
"I'd heard that fear expressed so many times from the beginning of my childhood. I thought now about my own relationship to money. The car I was driving was rented. I didn't want to own one....Underneath all of it, perhaps I didn't really want to have more than my parents had." [79]

THE POWERLESSNESS OF UNAWARENESS

There are five problems with remaining unaware:

1.   Our options are limited or even non-existent. Being unaware makes us think we are powerless. We get hooked by a trauma that hypnotizes us. This unconscious trauma is linked to certain situations or people, and when they are present we act automatically. We are victimized by unconscious memories that were not processed or understood, and by issues that remain unresolved.

2.   The more unaware we are, the more we "Act Out."

3.   We cannot heal what is unconscious. The unhappiness we experience today is left over pain from yesterday.

4.   Being unaware expends energy. Energy is the life force that keep us alive. The quality of life depends on how much energy we have to expend. If we spend the majority of our life force maintaining false belief systems, then we have less life force to live nourishing,

178

productive, rewarding, satisfying lives.

5. We continue behaving out of habit. We become extremely time incompetent. We tune out to ourselves. We can be sick and not notice until the situation is critical. We develop a way of being, a life style, a way of taking in a situation based on our role modeling, rewards, or punishments just the way we did as children.

We cannot heal what is not conscious. Our job is, therefore, to become aware. We must make the secrets conscious.

"If you think you can do a thing,
or think you can't do a thing,
you're right."
—Henry Ford

THE STAGES OF CHANGE

"Nothing endures but change."
—Heraclitus

"There is nothing in this world constant
but inconstancy."
—Jonathan Swift

Loss is loss. Change is loss.

Death, divorce, job loss or other dramatic changes are obvious kinds of losses. It is distressing to lose tangible possessions like money, a watch, or a car. It feels unbearably painful to lose a loved one--or a home. But change of any sort involves loss because--even when a change is positive--we leave behind some place, some person or thing that used to be a part of our lives. Changing parts of ourselves can be even more life-altering and painful.

Figure 7

THE BEHAVIORAL BAROMETER

CHOICE

CONSCIOUS

ACCEPTANCE
Choosing to	• Approachable
Optimistic	• Acceptable
Adaptable	• Worthy
Deserving	• Open

ANTAGONISM
Attacked	• Bothered
Questioned	• Burdened
Annoyed	• Indignant
Opposing	• Inadequate

WILLING
Receptive	• Adequate
Prepared	• Answerable
Encouraging	• Refreshed
Invigorated	• Aware

ANGER
Incensed	• Furious
Over-wrought	• Fuming
Seething	• Firey
Belligerent	• Hysterical

INTEREST
Fascinated	• Tuned-in
Needed	• Welcomed
Understanding	• Appreciated
Essential	• Caring

RESENTMENT
Hurt	• Embarrassed
Wounded	• Used/abused
Unappreciated	• Rejected
Dumb	• Offended

SUBCONSCIOUS

ENTHUSIASM
Amused	• Jubilant
Admirable	• Attractive
Delighted	• Excited
Alive	• Trusting

HOSTILITY
Trapped	• Picked-on
Put-upon	• Frustrated
Deprived	• Sarcastic
Vindictive	• With-holding

ASSURANCE
Motivated	• Daring
Protected	• Bold
Brave	• Considered
Affectionate	• Proud

FEAR OF LOSS
Let-down	• Not-heard
Bitter	• Disappointed
Threatened	• Over-looked
Frightened	• Unwelcome

EQUALITY
Lucky	• Co-operative
Involved	• Purposeful
Reliable	• Concerned
Sincere	• Productive

GRIEF AND GUILT
Betrayed	• Conquered
Discouraged	• Unacceptable
Self-punishing	• Despondent
Defeated	• Ruined

BODY

ATTUNEMENT
In tune with	• Congruent
In balance	• Creative
Perceptive	• Appreciative
Tender	• Gentle

INDIFFERENCE
Pessimistic	• Immobilized
Rigid	• Numb
Stagnant	• Unfeeling
Destructive	• Disconnected

ONENESS
Quiet	• Safe
Calm	• At peace
Unified	• Completed
Fulfilled	• At-one-ment

SEPARATION
Uncared for	• Unloved
Unacceptable	• Loveless/unlovable
Unimportant	• Melancholy
Morbid	• Deserted

CHOICE

Copyright © 1986
Three In One Concepts, Inc.
2018 West Burbank Boulevard - Suite A
Burbank, CA 91506
818 841-4786

The BEHAVIORAL BAROMETER is used in Three In One Concepts
Identification and Defusion programs.

PROCESSING LOSS

In numerous articles, lectures and books on dying, Kubler-Ross identifies the five emotional stages of accepting loss as denial, anger, bargaining, depression and acceptance. Her description has helped millions of individuals become aware of the process of letting go--not only of life itself, but of anything that must be left behind or changed. 80

Expanding on Kubler-Ross, Gary Emery, in his book, *Own Your Own Life,* has identified sub-parts of these stages. Within denial, there is first non-awareness and then disbelief. Part of bargaining is the avoidance of the anxiety caused by feeling out of control. 81

THE BEHAVIORS OF PROCESSING LOSS

An excellent model of the changes during the stages of loss is the Behavioral Barometer developed by Gordon Stokes and Daniel Whiteside. It plots an individual's growth, beginning at denial (no choice) and moving toward a place of choice. The Behavioral Barometer illustrates the range of emotions that an individual experiences to reach awareness. The first automatic response is defensiveness, characterized by negative thoughts, feelings, and behavior--the unconscious choice when positive choice is too unfamiliar or unattainable. Once in defensive mode, we are halted in the process of change. 82

However, if we can recognize our defensive reactions and deal with the emotions that are covered by the defensive stance, then, most often, anger will emerge. Unfortunately, anger is often thought to be unacceptable, producing reactions that are hurtful, bad, or unseemly. Because society condemns anger (especially in women) and rarely rewards it, anger is an emotion frequently avoided or denied. Look at the right side of the Behavioral Barometer (Figure 7) under *Anger*. The emotions are incensed, over-wrought, seething, belligerent, furious, fuming, fiery and hysterical. Since these emotions are not

OK to express, look directly to the left side of the Barometer and see what we miss by denying the anger: receptivity, preparedness, encouragement, invigoration, feeling adequate, being answerable, being refreshed and *being aware*. This seems devastating. What a price to pay! But now look down to the area titled *Separation* and check out the *actual price* we pay in our body when we don't express our anger: We feel uncared for, unacceptable, unimportant, morbid, unloved, loveless and unlovable, melancholy and deserted.

The bottom line is that unexpressed anger results in depression.

To avoid the pain of depression or the anxiety of processing a loss effectively, we can choose to return to unawareness. In *Further Along The Road Less Travelled,* Peck emphasizes the unfortunate fact that most of us leave this earth in the state of denial, not allowing ourselves to express or deal with anger. 83

Change is one of the losses that requires the painful breakthrough past defensiveness into anger.

THE REQUIREMENTS OF CHANGE

What is required of us to change, and what are the signs of readiness? What does change cost?

In *On Becoming A Person,* the renowned psychotherapist of the 1960s, Carl Rogers described our experience of change as from fixity to changingness, from rigid structure to flow, and from survival mode to self-in-process. 84 During years of observing a wide variety of people, personalities and problems, I have observed a similar process of change in my clients.

The following sketch is a way to visualize each of the stages. Each stage can be thought about in terms of "ease of movement." Stage One is a very heavy, immoveable rock. Stage Two is a large, 80 inch round pot, moveable but with great care and difficulty. Stage Three is a basketball that has a way to be played with and, with practice can be directed. Stage Four is a beach ball, without a way to be played with but easily bounced about. Stage Five is a balloon with ease of movement. Stage Six is a helium balloon, soaring. Stage Seven has no boundary, free like the air.

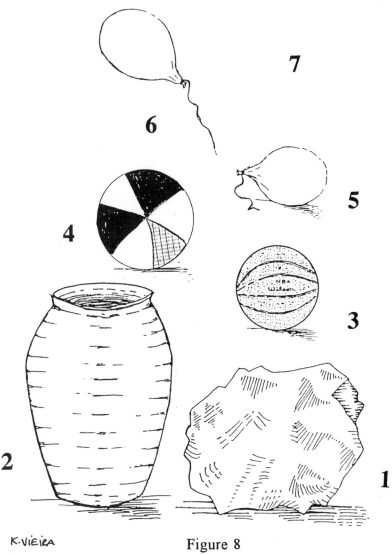

K·VIEIRA

Figure 8
Visualizing movement upward

Each stage requires a bit of the qualities of the next stage in order to move there. The following lists what is needed in one stage in order to move up the ladder of change:

Stage One, the Anti-Social Stage needs feeling fully received.

Stage Two, the Rule-Following Stage needs feeling miserable.

Stage Three, the Truth-Seeking Stage needs awareness.

Stage Four, the Responsible Stage needs introspection.

Stage Five, the Introspective Stage needs resolution of unresolved issues.

Stage Six, the Flowing Stage needs continued curiosity and willingness.

STAGE ONE
The Antisocial Stage

In Stage One, we are rigid and react reflexively to almost all situations. We see no alternative choices nor are we able to consider other options. We continue to act as we have always acted, without benefiting from experience. Our decision is "my way or the highway!" We are self-righteous and highly defensive and our intentions or needs supersede those of everyone else.

We seem remote, even to our own personal experiences. We assume no responsibility for our problems and see no need to change. If a problem cannot be denied, we blame it on someone else.

We neither recognize or seek feelings. If feelings are encountered, they are denied or avoided. We have no awareness or introspection nor do we care to have any. Close relationships and communication are perceived as dangerous, ridiculous, or a waste of time. We avoid feelings in any form.

Television's classic character, Archie Bunker, personifies the first stage. The mythical Narcissus is another personification of Stage One. Narcissus' symptom is "a self-absorption and containment that allows no connections of the heart. He is hard as a rock and repels all approaches of love. Obsessive, but not genuine, self-love leaves no room for intimacy with another....the narcissistic person becomes fixed on a single idea of who he is, and other possibilities are automatically rejected." [86] We are narcissistic because we are desperately trying to find self-acceptance within ourself since we cannot find it anywhere else.

Stage One characteristics can be seen on the Behavioral Barometer (figure 7) in the area of *Indifference, Separation* and *No Choice*. In a Johari Window, there is little area of free activity (Quadrant I.) On Maslow's Hierarchy of Needs, the needs are on the survival level.

Figure 9
Johari Window for Stage One

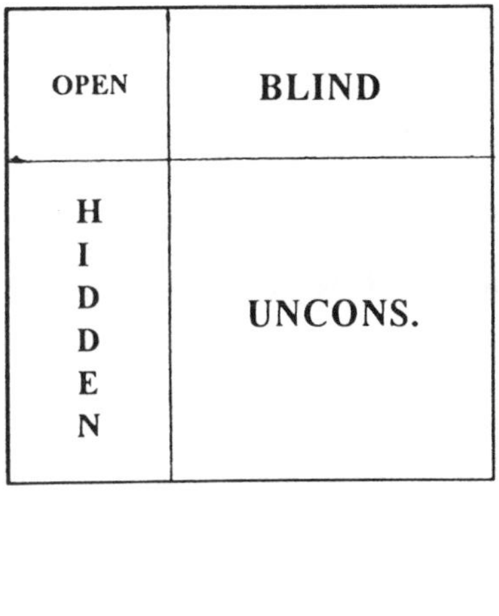

OPEN	BLIND
H I D D E N	UNCONS.

How can we emerge from Stage One? One widely-accepted psychological test and analysis, the Minnesota Multiphasic Personality Inventory, (or MMPI), refutes the possibility that someone in Stage One can change. The MMPI describes these individuals as having rigid personalities who probably would not seek help. It further proposes that should these people be forced to attend sessions geared toward helping them change, they would be unlikely to return.
87

Betty went long, but her child was never fully received.

The strongest motivation for getting out of the uncompromising position of Stage One seems to be our need to "feel received." The feeling of being "received" is the sense of feeling valued, safe, and understood. A psychotherapist's empathy may provide the opportunity for us in Stage One to feel received, should we ever seek help. Rogers makes this comment about the experience:

> We seem to know very little about how to provide the experience of being received for the person in the first stage, but it is occasionally achieved in play or group therapy where the person can be exposed to a receiving climate, without himself having to take any initiative, for a long enough time to experience himself *as received*. [88]

SECOND STAGE
The Rule-Following Stage

When we can tolerate the idea that someone else's behavior is not caused directly by us, and recognize that we may have some responsibility for what happens to us, then we have advanced to Stage Two. We no longer demand that what we think is absolute. In this stage, we handle feelings in a remote, unowned way--so that they seem external, not personal. For example, if we were in Stage Two we would say, "My symptom is being very depressed." We would not say, "I am depressed."

At this stage, we link the genesis and attachment of feelings and behaviors to institutions. The institution might be family, community, school, church, society, the military, or even prison. God is seen as external--a punitive ruler and enforcer akin to Orwell's "big brother." In Stage Two we function well because we strictly adhere to rules, roles, and guidelines, but we remain in a place of *Grief and Guilt, Fear of Loss* and *Hostility* (Behavioral Barometer.) We are still governed by deficiency needs and we feel somewhat better about ourselves because we feel we belong and we have less need to hide ourselves.

If we feel received by a church, the military, or an entity as large as "society," then we diligently learn and follow the rules. Model prisoners who have been paroled are often back in their cells within a short time. They are labeled "institutional men" because they cannot effectively function without the

189

comprehensive structure of prison.

Charles Manson has been identified as an institutional man because he functions well inside prison. Should Manson return to society, he might be as dangerous as when he orchestrated the slaughter of several people in the 1970s.

How do we get from Stages One or Two to Stage Three? The primary motivator is misery--or at least extreme discomfort. If we remain in the survival mode of Stage One or Two, we are not aware that we have choices. Our survival still relies on fixed and rigid belief systems so that we are unaware that we have a problem. Fortunately, human nature can assist us in breaking through the paradox--by letting us feel we are missing fundamental conditions of life that nearly all human beings value as worthwhile.

No matter how inflexible we are, we (consciously or unconsciously) wish to be loved, to have friends, to keep a job, be productive, feel safe, live where we feel accepted, enjoy a sense of belonging and feel good about ourselves. When the absence of these fundamental states causes significant discomfort, we may seek more information about ourselves. Dissatisfaction must be strong enough to motivate us or there is little hope that we will emerge from the non-awareness of Stage One and Two.

The possibility of advancing to Stage Three also provides a powerful paradox:

How can we feel received without first resolving basic family issues, when resolving the issues *requires insight beyond Stage Two?*

In Stage One or Two we are not aware that our parenting was so dominating, intrusive, intimidating that we rarely, if ever, felt *fully received.* As adults, we still long for that approval--from parents or surrogate parents, be they spouses, friends, employers, the people we encounter every day at work, or in our personal life. To be able to resolve past issues, we need to be willing to risk *never* feeling received.

Mickey was a passive person who agreed to see me because his wife, Barbara, asked him to come. He insisted that he loved his wife very

190

much. He said his number one priority in life was to "make her happy." He could not understand why she feels unhappy, when he will do anything to help her. (Her every wish is his loving command.)

But Barbara is upset because Mickey does not make his own company a priority, and as a result, is not contributing to the family income. Instead, Mickey plays golf and religiously reads the entire daily newspaper. He schedules golf games three times a week, is never late for them, and is diligent in setting up foursomes for the group.

In an argument, Barbara pointed out how he sets priorities for playing golf and reading the newspaper, but not for his business. Mickey was devastated that he had made Barbara unhappy. He decided to stop reading his newspaper and developed a sciatic nerve problem in his leg. The pain prohibited him from hitting a golf ball (unconsciously giving him an excuse not to play golf). He had not been aware that he was living irresponsibly, and was determined to avoid further criticism from Barbara. He did not have a conscious awareness of reluctance not to be successful.

In exploring his history, it became apparent that he had been severely criticized all of his life. Because of this criticism, he had never advanced past his three- to six-year-old developmental stage of growth. His need for approval by his wife, friends, and co-workers took the place of his desperate need for approval from his parents. He never felt "fully received" by his parents, and upon marrying Barbara, he set up a marginal work ethic, so that he would constantly challenge Barbara's love for him by not performing to his capacity. When she questioned him, he felt instantly criticized and "unreceived."

Mickey's case is a good illustration of the paradox. He will advance to Stage Three only if he feels uncomfortable enough in his marriage or in his business. If Barbara leaves him, or continues to confront him, he may become miserable enough to question his present choices. But if Barbara accepts his childish needs for approval without accomplishment, he will continue to live in a manner that has no consequences, which relegates him to Stage Two. Mickey yearns to feel loved "no matter what," and if that need is fulfilled by his devoted spouse, a friend, or acquaintance, the good feeling (of being received "just as he is") will remove the discomfort needed to motivate him to want to move forward to Stage Three.

Awareness frees us to make new choices in relationships, judgements, actions, values, goals, and beliefs. If Mickey could become aware of his irresponsibility, his true nature could emerge and be modeled by new choices.

TRUE NATURE?

The true nature of human beings is frequently misunderstood as it relates to our ability to change. Can we change by willing it? The story of the frog and the scorpion illustrates the unhappy consequences of non-awareness and inability to change.

> The scorpion asks the frog to take him across the river. The frog declines, saying he fears that the scorpion will sting him. The scorpion promises not to sting the frog, declaring that it would not be in his own self-interest. So the frog agrees to the journey. Halfway across the river, the scorpion stings the frog, causing them both to drown. As they are going down, the frog asks the scorpion why he stung him. The scorpion answers, "It is just my nature."

The impulse to grow and become our own person exists in us as babies. All our basic needs (from survival to actualization) make up our human nature. Basic needs cannot be frustrated if human nature is to find expression and realization.

Only separation from our primary attachments (good or bad) allows us to find our true nature. The ability to remain non-defensive allows us to separate from the Stages One and Two.

To change, we must move beyond rationalizing that, "It's just the way I am," or "I'm only human." These defensive stances are not part of our basic nature. They are manifestations of a basic survival instinct to keep us safe from what we perceive as danger, attack, fear, loss of love, or annihilation.

A percentage of the population will always remain in Stage One or Two. Those who remain there will not read a book like the one you are reading, or attend conferences to learn about themselves. They will lead limited and unquestioning existences, repeating the mistakes that their parents made.

The first sign of movement toward Stage Three is a flicker of awareness, followed by disbelief or denial. Why? Because the state of *disbelief depends on not believing in something.* To say, "I don't believe that," requires acknowledgement of something we haven't heard before.

If the warning light on the dash board of our car indicates that our oil is low, we have to acknowledge that there is a problem. If we ignore it (Stage Two), then we will have a more serious problem. Smashing the red light with a hammer (Stage One) instead of recognizing it as the *sign* of a problem (not the problem itself), would create more problems. To say, "I don't see the red light flashing," is acknowledgement that the red light was seen.

At this stage it helps if we allow someone to help us explore our denial, defenses and disbelief. We must feel safe enough to ask, "It wasn't my fault, *was it*?" At this point, we can advance toward Stage Three. If we never ask the question and continue to believe "It wasn't my fault," we will not get beyond Stages One and Two.

When my friend said, "I won't be defensive anymore--I will be dominated and gouged," He heard his belief system "sneak out." Because of that insight he was able to move into Stage Three.

STAGE THREE
The Truth-seeking Stage

This stage will evolve only if we continue to "feel received." If we become defensive again, progress will stop and we will return to the survival mode of Stages One and Two.

In Stage Three we need to relax and feel good that "someone understands" or "at least that I am doing something about this." In this stage, we can

193

consider different members of our family and compare our qualities to theirs. We may decide that "I am just like my mother on this issue" or that "This is something my Uncle Jim would say." As we begin to explore, we will gain insight and recognize that these insights have meaning. We can recognize contradictions in our beliefs and actions. "That's just what I hate about my mother, and that's what I do with my own kids!" is an insight that was not possible until Stage Three.

Quincy wanted to investigate psychotherapy because he had lost all feelings for his wife. He moved out of their home and, because of limited finances, moved into his parents' home which he had left 20 years ago. He joined a therapy group, and soon realized that the way he perceived the world, was contrary to that of every other group member.

As Quincy continued living with his parents house, he began to see that he had "become his father" and perceived the world as pessimistically as his father did. He also recognized that he had married a woman with many of his mother's traits. This recognition formed the springboard to his growth process. The recognition made it possible for him to move to Stage Four.

Honey, I've become just like my mother.

In Stage Three we begin to recognize the *Antagonism, Anger* and *Resentment* on the Behavioral Barometer. We are much less blind to what is happening and why we are the way we are. We have less need to hide our feelings that heretofore have felt unacceptable.

STAGE FOUR
The Responsible Stage

Stage Four is the stage of change-readiness. In this stage we become aware that we are responsible for our own problems, and actively can do something to help ourselves. Asking "Why am I yelling at my kids like Mom yelled at me?" is the beginning of the end of an unresolved issue that repeatedly caused unconscious and automatic responses.

At this point a person might seek psychotherapy, attend conferences, awareness training or self-improvement seminars. Reading self-help books and self-awareness information may help us on our journey.

At Stage Four we make a connection between who we are today, and who we were made to be within our family of origin. We can recognize whether or not we have successfully separated from our parents' viewpoints or removed ourselves from the legacy of family dysfunction. With the ability to reflect and understand how certain issues caused our present problems, we have the option to resolve those problems.

We now know that the number of possibilities is much greater. We want to seek new options and be "at choice," finally mastering our own reality. We feel desire to explore our purpose for being here, and we hope that we can maximize our potential.

We have reached the stage in which *Acceptance, Willingness* and *Interest* on the Behavioral Barometer flourish. We have reached the level of satisfying needs beyond deficiency on Maslow's Hierarchy of Needs. Stage Four is a beginning.

STAGE FIVE
The Introspective Stage

In Stage Five, "Feelings are very close to being fully experienced. They 'bubble up,' and 'seep through.'" [89]

We begin to accept the quality of our feelings and believe we matter to ourselves and others. We feel we belong and are accepted in our expressions and behavior. In this stage it is important for "the real me" to become known. A degree of spontaneity becomes normal. Introspection is more frequent. Looking into why behavior is the way it is becomes possible, and choice becomes an option for the first time. We might feel great and at the same time, a bit apprehensive about the new feelings.

Rogers states:

> This phase is several hundred psychological miles from the first stage described. Here many aspects of the client are in flow, as against the rigidity of the first stage. He is very much closer to his organic being, which is always in process. He is much closer to being in the flow of his feelings. His constructions of experience are decidedly loosened and repeatedly being tested against referents and evidence within the without. Experience is much more highly differentiated, and thus internal communication, already flowing, can be much more exact." [90]

This is the stage when self-help books are the most useful, when psychotherapy is most beneficial, and when change, through new information, is fruitful. This is the stage where we not only actively seek new information, but activate new behaviors. On the Behavioral Barometer we feel *Enthusiastic, Assurance* and *Equality*. We may feel that we have arrived!

STAGE SIX
The Flowing Stage

At this stage, previously held belief systems no longer hold us captive. The present is allowed to be experienced as the present without the baggage of the past. This stage is a further enhancement of Stage Five. Once we reach this stage *it is unlikely that we will ever return to any of the previous stages.* In this stage we have become individuated--our own person. We are no longer stuck. Feelings flow because of a certainty that they are valuable to ourselves and others. We immediately relate to our experiences and naturally flow to find where new experiences lead.

The incongruence between experience and awareness is vividly experienced as it disappears into congruence. Defense mechanisms are not needed. The *sensor/censor* of our childhood, (the one we needed by our ego to survive), has no serviceable purpose. Freed from attachment issues we are individuated and we are ready to experience life at its fullest. We feel *Attuned* and *At-One-ment* (Behavioral Barometer.)

Figure 10
Johari Window for Stage Five, Six and Seven

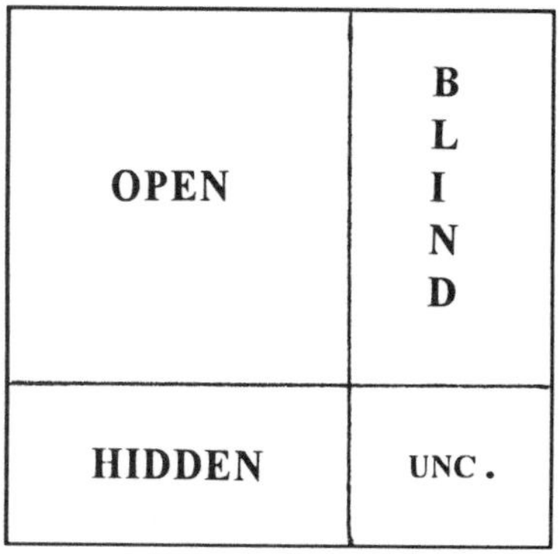

OPEN	**B L I N D**
HIDDEN	UNC.

STAGE SEVEN
The Interdependent Stage

The highlight of this stage is the ultimate trust in our own process. Trust, autonomy, initiative, a sense of individuation, and the capacity for intimacy are established. We reach the favorable outcomes seen in Table 1. Close, healthy personal relationships are a vital part of our lives.

Stephen Covey describes interdependency as a way of being in which we are not dependent on others, not independent of others, but connected in such a way that we value others' presence in our lives, realizing that what they offer can only enhance our lives. [91]

Life seems rich in each of its experiences and it is modified by each new experience.

> "Internal communication is clear, with feelings and symbols well-matched, and fresh terms for new feelings. There is the experiencing of effective choice, of new ways of being." [92]

Being aware that these seven stages exist can help us locate where we are on the pathway of life.

INTROSPECTION
THE KEY TO AWARENESS

"Being alive is the habit of choosing your response--
the habit of awareness that I'm a separate person
from all that has happened to me including
all my feelings, my moods, my genetic makeup ..."
—Stephen Covey

"...we stare backwards into time,
and continue to find new plots, new patterns.
These thoughts now hold no fear
because we have thought them....
It is the unthought that hold us in thrall...
what we do not know is what we most know."
—Margaret Drabble

Without introspection, there can be no awareness. Introspection is the thinking about our own thoughts and sensations. It is a way in which we look into our selves, turning our thoughts inward and examining our feelings. We can be introspective about our past, present and future. All three viewpoints are important in introspection in examining our lives with regard to how we use time, receive payoffs, relate to others, adhere to unwritten contracts, and allow society's belief systems to influence us.

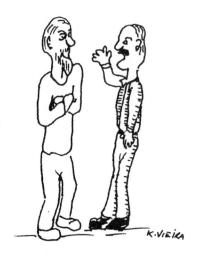

"Do you examine yourself? My doctor told me
I couldn't introspect without a license."

HOW TO BEGIN TO BE INTROSPECTIVE

One way to begin being introspective is to record all powerful personal feelings as we become aware of them. We can notice when we hear meaningful words, when we cry at the movies, when we feel touched, angered, defensive, or fearful. We must become aware of and record feelings we tend not to reveal. These might include feelings of anxiety, inadequacy, self-doubt, anger, fear, guilt, sadness, hostility, love, or hope.

Recently, I attended a film class, in which we discussed the movie *Rocky*. The instructor explained that the inciting incident, that made the movie great occurred when Rocky knew he couldn't win, but knew he would go the distance. During the discussion, I suddenly felt choked with emotion, but fought to hide the tears. Then I became uneasy feeling that someone would see my reaction. I was sitting in a classroom just hearing about the story, yet it affected me the same way it had affected the movie's original audiences.

When I returned home I wrote down how I felt about this incident. In the background was a belief system instilled in me by my father. He said, "Anything you want you can have, if you work for it." I wanted to believe this for his sake, as well as my own. But I now believe that the maxim is not entirely true. There are many variables that intervene to decide my fate and affect my desires.

For example, I looked forward to having children. When I underwent surgery to make that possible, my body went into menopause instead. I learned then that there are some things we cannot have regardless of how hard we work or how much we want them. The emotional reaction to seeing *Rocky* came from the sadness that this core belief system no longer existed for me--it was a mourning.

The fact that some things are not possible is now acceptable to me. Knowing what I want, being willing to work toward a goal, and doing my best gives me great pleasure. When I realize that I can change direction and find other interests, for my efforts, I feel gratified. My old belief system was supposed to assure me of control over my fate. Instead, it gave me unrealistic expectations that did not serve me well. By having this awareness, and by separating from it, I now have other options.

We need to explore those secrets within ourselves without becoming blocked, anxious, or confused. We say we want greater meaning in our lives and deeper relationships, yet we are defeated by the roles we play and thwarted by games imposed on us by society. Introspection is our ticket to awareness and the option to change.

THE THREE ASPECTS OF INTROSPECTION

The first and most important aspect of introspection, is knowing what we *are doing* in the present. It is the *how* of what we are doing now in contrast to *why* we are doing it or whether we want to continue doing it. Only with awareness of where we are, is it possible for us to be move beyond somewhere else.

The second aspect of introspection is thinking about what happened in the past. We look *to see what happened* in the past to make us who we are in the present. This is the way that unresolved issues are discovered so that we do not repeat them. It is this aspect of introspection that allows us to be free in the present by understanding the past.

The third aspect of introspection is enhancing our future by learning from experiences of the past. This aspect of introspection allows us to know that we can be different in the future, by seeing what we have done in the past and doing things differently. With introspection we can assume responsibility for our own behavior and acknowledge our own power to make change.

IMPORTANCE OF TIME-COMPETENCE

One way to avoid being aware is to function "on automatic behavior." Then we act out of habit, not awareness. We become time-incompetent, functioning (not really living) today the way we did through yesterday. We can become sick and not know it, paying no attention to obvious signs until our bodies are in crisis.

> For weeks, Bill had planned how to approach his boss for a raise. He practiced what he would say until he was able to imagine himself emerging victorious. Finally, he went to see his boss. As Bill began to set the stage for his "speech," his boss interrupted him saying, "Before you tell me why you're here, I want to commend you on the great job you are doing and let you know that I'm giving you a raise." The raise was larger than Bill had hoped, but he left the office feeling "ripped off"

because he didn't get a chance to play out the scene he'd rehearsed.

Bill had made a "Jill" story, with idealized goals, plans, expectations, and predictions. He got so caught up in his future that he missed the joy of what happened as it happened in the present. He was time-Incompetent.

Other examples of time-incompetence are nursing wounds of the past ("I can't stand the hurt of another relationship--I always get dumped.") feeling regretful for a past action ("I shouldn't have quit my job. It was the best job I ever had"), and feeling guilty ("If only I hadn't left him alone, he'd be alive today.")

In instances like these we live without being introspective. We squander our *now* experiences by not being *present*. Instead, we live or relive the *past*.

We can also be time-incompetent by living in the future. We plan for "when we retire," "when he calls," "when I get this job," or "as soon as I graduate."

> A neighbor of mine had a stroke. From that moment he bemoaned his fate, focusing on dying and never enjoying the remaining *ten* years of his life. He outlived other, seemingly healthier, family members, neighbors and friends.

A time-competent person lives primarily in the present, with awareness, contact, and a full range of sensations and feelings in the now. One of Maslow's criteria for self-actualization (the highest rung of the hierarchy of needs), is time-competence, focusing in the present. Maslow studied healthy, functional persons who felt safe, unanxious, accepted, loved, loving, respect-worthy, and respected. He discovered that time-competent people experienced more happiness, serenity, and richness of their inner life. [93]

If this is true, why aren't we all more time-competent? Why aren't we willing to be happier? Thousands of pages have been written on this subject. Thoreau wrote, "Most of us will have so little respect for life that we will reach the point of death without ever having lived at all." Erich Fromm echoed this fear when he stated that, "The greatest tragedy of life is the fact that most human beings die before they are fully born."

We do not fully live in the present because we are not introspective. We were not taught or encouraged to be introspective. As children, we had to accept what was given to us. Typically, we did not wonder, "Is this a healthy way for my parents to treat me?" We turned off our introspection and accepted what was happening as right. As adults, we easily slip into "automatic" and repeat past behaviors without examining whether of not that behavior serves us in the present. Leo Buscaglia, in his excellent book, *Personhood* states, "I cannot understand why, given a choice between joy and despair, people will so often choose despair." [94]

It is because it is all we know!

PAYOFFS

We have an investment in holding onto behavior, and beliefs that have a payoff, regardless of how functional that payoff has been in the past or continues to be in the present. We needed the payoff at one time. Now the payoff is *just what we do*.

We may need the payoff of getting attention or feeling safe and secure but our means of getting the old payoff may not be effective any longer. We may need to examine if we still need that payoff and, if we do, can we discover a new behavior that is more effective that has the same payoff.

Most of us respond to our environment with a collection of automatic responses that once brought us favorable results. Many times, as we grow up, these automatic responses are no longer appropriate and, in fact, become counter-productive. Giving up old payoffs can be cause anxiety. If we learned to get attention by asking questions, washing mother's car, being smart, or by being good at being bad, our defenses will protect that attention-getting device. Without that "way," we are convinced that we will get no attention at all.

> A little boy on a train kept saying, "Boy, am I thirsty." The man sitting next to him decided to get him a glass of water. As the man sat back down again the little boy said, "Boy, was I thirsty."

> A woman boarded a bus, looked at the driver and asked if he is Polish.

204

The driver said, "No, lady, I'm not Polish." The next day she again boarded the bus, sat down and asked the driver, "Excuse me sir, but are you sure you're not Polish?" Out of frustration, the driver said, "OK, I'm Polish." The woman smiled and said, "That's funny. You don't look Polish." [95]

We develop a lifestyle based on what happened to us in the past. We developed coping styles that had payoffs appropriate to a time in our past. These coping styles may no longer serve us well.

With introspection we become aware of the payoffs. We enter Stage Four and Stage Five and examine our core belief systems. We "explode into awareness" because we are in touch with our own feelings, values, and behavior. We are in the continuum of awareness, and we discover our self-in-process. The payoffs we now require differ greatly from payoffs we needed in the past. One of the payoffs we seek is meaningful relationships in our lives.

HOW "DEEPLY" ARE WE WILLING TO RELATE TO OTHERS?

Think of the people in our lives who operate primarily on cliches. These are the people who say "Hi, how are you?" and then respond, "Great!" regardless of your answer. I call these people "weather discussers." These are the people who talk at you, but not with you. The cliche people are at Stage One in the growth process. They don't see the need for relating in any other way.

A "deeper" level of relating, but one that still deprives us of awareness is needing "roles." We use roles--of what we do, what we have or who we know--to prove we are OK. Granted, we adjust to roles appropriate for our careers, responsibilities and relationships. But when we need a role in order to feel worthy, the "who" we are seems not to matter.

Like the wealthy character in the nostalgic movies who fears he will loose all his "friends" if he becomes penniless. His friends depend on the prestigious or status role he served them. He fears losing identity (his very being) if he removes his disguise. People to whom the role means everything are stuck in Stage Two.

When the opinions of others is our primary concern, we get stuck being co-dependent and dysfunctional. It is a powerless position, totally out of our awareness.

The world conspires to assist us in role-playing. For example, in sports, in the film business, in the community, the "famous" people are invited to social functions. "Lesser" persons may be left out.

When we come out of our roles, our defense mechanisms "fire up" because we feel anxious and uncomfortable, like "fish out of water." We feel distressed. We may become angry, distance ourselves, blame others, withdraw internally, or get depressed. We may retreat into denial in order to avoid the experience of emptiness, a nothingness, or a void in which we feel stuck. We hate ourselves for being in this place. We feel inadequate as human beings. Life seems to be at an impasse.

To emerge from the impasse we must fill in the gaps in our personalities. We are good at avoiding or denying the holes in our personalities. We pretend they are not there or we project what is missing onto others. For the most part the missing parts are unconscious.

The purpose of becoming aware is get out of the impasse, to become whole, to reclaim the parts of ourselves that we have denied and/or never known. *Being aware* is the only way to maximize our potential.

In the process of becoming aware we mobilize our own resources, we begin to take back parts we gave away or disowned because they displeased someone or were never developed. When we become aware of all our parts, our whole being can be active and "in-process."

"I don't think Joe is all together. He has major gaps in his personality."

Think about being a cake. The cake is made up of numerous ingredients, the majority of which, if tasted individually, would not be appealing. The flour, shortening, vanilla, baking powder and so on are essential to make a cake. Each individual cake is made up of some of the same, but many different ingredients. Each ingredient is essential. If we leave out baking soda or vanilla or an ingredient that the recipe calls for, the cake will not be right. We need to accept all the parts of the cake--regardless of how they taste individually--for the cake to be whole, and as it was intended.

We are like the cake, we need to have all the ingredients we were meant to have and not judge them individually as to whether or not to include them in our personality.

FOCUS ON SOCIETY'S BELIEF SYSTEMS

We are often divided against ourselves by the game society imposes on us. What we say we need or want is often thwarted by society's demand for us to maintain the appropriate front for society's own sake. A glaring example of society's blindness to various human conditions is seen in its resistance to understand and accept the homosexual community. Another is the prejudice against anyone who chooses a life that is "out of the norm."

> Stephanie is a psychologist who is manic depressive. Manic depression is a disorder which causes severe mood swings, unless managed by therapeutic doses of lithium. Throughout graduate school Stephanie struggled with her illness. She began taking lithium after reading about the illness and soon felt much better without the terrifying spells of chemical imbalance. When people hear her describe how she suffered from manic-depression, they feel very uncomfortable. One friend asked how she expected to help others, if she herself was mentally ill.

Society is ill-informed about chemical imbalances and psychoactive drugs--and quick to judge what it does not understand. People with properly treated chemical imbalances can function as well as people without the imbalances.

When we face the reality of our lives--who we are, how we feel, and what we need, we encounter society's own belief systems. We are each caught in the continuous battle with our own culture. Culture doesn't confront us as a single adversary but challenges us through the roles people play in our lives. Culture acts upon us through our family, friends, business associates, and even our casual acquaintances. These persons determine the "rules" which society imposes upon us in order to make "everyone" comfortable.

When we are validated by society--that is, when we fit within the norm of "doing" what is expected, we do not "make waves" or disrupt the status-quo. Therefore society leaves us alone because we are not causing any discomfort. It is important and healthy to question ourselves, when what we are doing to "fit into society," does not seem to reflect our internal self.

When I was growing up in the 1960's, I reacted negatively to the news that Richard Allpert, a Stanford professor, gave up his "acceptable" position to become Ram Dass, a hippie of sorts who meditated and spoke of truths he had discovered. I was horrified and in awe. I couldn't understand how a college professor could want to do something like that.

More recently, Shirley MacLaine revealed her many past lives. [96] Many people who have changed their belief systems changed their lives, and in some cases the lives of others. Among them are Gandhi, Martin Luther King, Jr., Brian Weiss (who wrote *Many Lives, Many Masters)* [97], and John Thie (who launched a layman's health-care system in *Touch For Health.)* [98]

People who dare to confront existing belief systems take a huge chance. They dare to live beyond a facade that makes others comfortable. Too often we protect our image in order to fit within society's acceptable boundaries. Too often, others avoid talking to us about such things as doubts, fears, and inadequacies. Our masks remove us from experiencing our inner reality. We become incongruent and fake. We deny who we are and settle for who others think we should be, so that we (and they) can feel "comfortable."

UNWRITTEN CONTRACTS

I remember Fritz Perls telling a large audience at Esalen in the 1960's, "Get rid of your pile of shoulds!" If we don't, we tend to protect our pile and other people's piles as well. There seems to be a rule among those of us who hide ourselves. The rule is, "If I am hiding and you know it and you won't call me on it, then I won't call you on what you are hiding either" (Quadrant III rule-- Chapter 8). This pact among people is an *unwritten contract*.

I find that in almost any mix of people, the Quadrant III rule applies. When members of a therapy group begin to collude in not confronting one another and keeping feelings to themselves, all group work stops. The defense system within the group kills any possibility of change for its members. Similarly, when the group does not challenge the isolation of a member, isolation permeates the group. That acceptance, harmful though it might be, becomes a condition of reality.

If no one notices or confronts us on a particular issue and we don't reveal it, that issue does not exist for us. What we see or say repeatedly will manifest itself in our life.

> Max is a relatively wealthy man. Over the years Max paid for most of the lunch and bar tabs for his friend Len, who accepted Max's generosity. When Len got married, he had a party and asked Max to bring something to a "pot luck." Max chose not to attend, and Len was so angry that he ended the friendship. Perhaps Len expected Max to continue to extend his generosity by catering the event.

This situation is not an uncommon example of how unstated agreements and assumptions can explode and hurt people. The contract between Max and Len was that Max took care of Len. They colluded to hide the fact that Max's "generosity" got in the way of dealing with Len not paying his way in the friendship. In order to avoid feeling guilty, Len made Max "the bad guy."

Max could have informed Len that he didn't want to "carry Len." Instead, throughout the friendship, he rationalized the situation by thinking, "I've got more money, so I shouldn't resent paying for everything." Len could have told Max, "I feel funny when you pay for everything. I feel that you don't respect me." If either friend had revealed his feelings, their friendship would have had a more honest contract that was more nourishing for both.

Relationships that work, in therapy or not, are those in which each person is allowed to explore and "try on" new rules and behaviors, to explore *contracts* that have been a unstated. Each person, within a safe relationship, should be free to examine previously held *contracts* without the fear that the evaluation will meet with criticism or rejection.

Maslow's study of healthy people concluded that healthy, happy people are not split between inner and outer--between what they feel inside and what others know about them. At this level of self-actualization, Maslow found that "differences become resolved, opposites are seen as unities, work becomes play, duty is pleasant, and pleasure becomes the fulfillment of duty." [99]

We experience the greatest psychological pain when there is an incongruity between the "who" that we project and "who" we really are, of how we see ourselves, and how others see us. When we are congruent and feel understood, we feel at one. We are at peace.

> One of my most painful experiences occurred when I competed in tennis. I am an extroverted, competitive and excitable type of person. My partner is a very popular, gentle lady. As partners, we won many tournaments, yet she eventually decided she did not want to play with me. When I asked her about her decision, she explained that when we won a match I jumped up and down and was so visibly happy that it embarrassed her.

My belief system allowed me to show how good I felt about winning. Her belief system caused her to feel embarrassed by my enthusiasm, because she felt my exuberance made the other team feel doubly bad about losing. Her belief system told her that hurting others in any way was wrong. I believe she felt just as happy (inside) about winning as I did. Neither of us was right or wrong. We were just different, so different that she would feel disloyal to herself if she were to play with me. I tried to hide my enthusiasm at the end of matches but I felt constricted and unauthentic. Behaving "with her values" made me feel disloyal to my inner working. Our belief systems conflicted, and we did not play together again.

She saw me as an uncaring person. The incongruity about the way she saw me and the way that I saw myself caused me a great deal of pain. Interestingly, I have since lost the incentive to play tennis. I will need to be introspective to find out whether the pain of this incongruity had anything to do with my decision to quit playing tennis. Perhaps I just lost interest in the sport; as Freud said, "Sometimes a cigar is just a cigar!"

SEPARATION
THE KEY TO INDIVIDUATION

"I need and want to make a disclaimer: When I talk about mother or primary care giver, I do not mean *real mother* but mother *as an experience* that did or did not or could not meet the child's needs."

—Larry Hedges

"Give your child roots and wings,
not loot and things"

—Denis Waitley

"Parenting is the only relationship
whose success is measured by the
quality of separation."

—Sidney Lumet

"The wounded child cannot be healed
if parents continue to be idealized."

—John Bradshaw

Numerous authors including Erikson, Winnecott, Mahler, Freud and Hedges have written about the first years of life and "normal development" needed for a child to lead to a healthy and productive life. The problem lies not in describing what "normal development" is, but in accomplishing it.

Tony Robbins, author of *Unlimited Power*, writes that 80 percent of today's families are dysfunctional. [100] I believe the percentage is so high because today's children are not allowed to separate from their families of origin. Dysfunctional, then, means that the phase of attachment has been extended beyond the normal limits and therefore separation has not been accomplished in a manner that allows for the self-in-process to fully flourish. The child in us must be able to let go of the past in order to take hold of the present and future.

DEFINING INDIVIDUATION

Individuation is the emergence of a person in his or her own right who is able to search for and attain a meaningful life. A person who attains individuation can initiate and sustain a process of individual growth toward ever-increasing personal competence and adequacy--free from endless repetition of unresolved issues of the past.

Individuation needs to happen at the third juncture of separation which occurs between three and 18 years of age. Without this final separation at 18 years of age, individuation is not possible. The situations below describe the three basic conditions that prevent separation from taking place:

1. When the fine line between giving too much and not giving enough is violated.

2. When parents need us for their own gratification.

3. When we must focus on our parents' needs rather than our own. This includes when we cannot surpass our parents, when we cannot

be happier than our parents, and when we become emotional surrogate spouses for our parent.

THE FINE LINE BETWEEN GIVING TOO MUCH AND NOT GIVING ENOUGH

We need our parents consistent support to help us develop trust, to feel loved and cared for, but we must not be so overindulged that we cannot achieve autonomy.

If we, as children, want something for the sake of wanting it (as all children do) and we are indulged every time, we will not learn the essential process of delaying gratification. If, on the other hand, something that is appropriate to need and want, is denied us, for the sake of denying it (or withheld from us out of neglect) we learn that our needs are not important.

Maintaining the fine line between giving too much and not giving enough can be compared to learning how to swim. If every time we took an awkward stroke, our parent pulled us out of the water, we would never learn to swim. On the other hand, if we needed assistance and our parent did not rescue us before we were terrorized with fear of drowning or being in actual danger, then we would probably not learn to swim either.

There is a delicate distinction between getting help too soon (so that we do not get a chance to develop new skills) and not getting help soon enough (so that we feel too afraid to try new things). Finding this fine line is essential.

> My husband and I once were given a new born kitten. We fed her milk with an eye dropper and raised her indoors. Before she was old enough, she wandered outside and was taken away by a coyote. Since she had never been allowed to *fend for herself,* she was unable to take care of herself when she was on her own.

Children who are granted every wish and not allowed to learn to accept responsibility for themselves will have to be "kept indoors," like the kitten, or

215

they too will be prey to a world in which they are not prepared to survive in.

Continual gratification prohibits optimal levels of frustration and socialization. As long as immediate gratification continues, we never learn to experience being "on our own," and we never separate from the source of that gratification (which in most cases, is our parents). If we are gratified all the time, we come to rely on that gratification (rather than ourselves) as the source of our needs being met. Any absence of a gratifying parent, then, is experienced as abandonment, and that imagined separation feels like annihilation.

For us to develop normally and successfully separate from our parents, we must practice the know-how to use restraint and know that there are consequences for behaviors that are inappropriate. For example, we learn that we may not have all the cookies in the cookie jar (restraint) because, if we eat all of them, we will get sick (consequences).

On the other hand, when our legitimate needs are neglected, we develop what psychologists call "learned helplessness," which is the belief that we are at the mercy of external forces, that we no longer have control over what happens to us.

In a well-known experiment, two groups of college students were studied to demonstrate learned helplessness. Both groups were exposed to a very loud noise in a room from which they could not escape. The first group was given a button that would shut off the loud noise. The second group had no way to stop the noise. In the second phase of the experiment, the same groups were put into different rooms. Both rooms were equipped with a button that would turn off the noise. The first group looked for the button and used it. The second group, which had no way to turn off the noise in the first experiment, did not even bother to look.

We who have not been allowed to take responsibility for our lives, learn to be helpless. We aren't given the opportunity to be productive on our own, and we are left with an emptiness inside of us. Until our loss is grieved and resolved, we will feel helpless and worthless.

     I once heard a lovely story about a little boy who found a caterpillar lying on the sidewalk. The boy picked it up and placed it gently on his jacket. Upon arriving home, he showed his mother the caterpillar and asked if she thought it would live. She put it on a bed of leaves and grass, and told her son he could possibly observe the caterpillar turn into a butterfly. The boy, of course, was thrilled, and eagerly watched it develop. Gradually the caterpillar began the transformation from cocoon to butterfly. At one point in its struggle to free itself from its cocooned body, the caterpillar seemed to falter and stopped moving altogether. The horrified boy thought that one thread seemed tighter than all the others and thinking that the struggle had been too difficult for the caterpillar, snipped the tight thread with a tiny pair of scissors. Sure enough, the caterpillar started moving inside the cocoon. Within a few days, the butterfly emerged from the tiny cocoon, but the butterfly had only one wing. The little boy subsequently learned that the caterpillar develops his butterfly's wings by struggling.

Over-loving, over-giving, well-intentioned parents sometimes interfere with a struggle that develops our wings.

WHEN PARENTS NEED US
FOR THEIR OWN GRATIFICATION

When parents depend on us to make them feel "like good parents" they create an abnormal environment which keeps us attached to them in a dysfunctional way.

Parenting is an awesome responsibility. It is frequently a thankless job. Whether or not it is "rewarding" depends on what kind of job is done, as with any other job. Parents should not need us to appreciate them ("You should ... because of all I do for you!"), to like them ("Do you love mommy?" or "Then I hate you too."), to be there for them ("You seem to like your friends more than you like your family"), or support them ("You're my little man." "You can be the daddy now.", "She's like a little mommy. She can do all the things I do...").

217

Diane was notified late one summer that she had been accepted at the university. In order for Diane to try out for cheerleading (which she had enjoyed in high school), she had to arrive at the university the next day. Diane's parents were on holiday, and when they heard the news, they decided to remain at the resort, as planned. Diane was in a panic about how to get up to the university in time for the tryouts. She decided to rent a U-Haul and take herself and her furniture to the university. When her parents found out, they were irate. They felt that *they* had been denied the experience of placing their child in college. Diane was seen by her parents as betraying *their* needs.

Joseph Kennedy, a narcissistic patriarch, who was not able to fulfill his own political desires, pushed his children to seek the positions he wanted. No one will ever know what Joseph Kennedy, Jr. (who died early in life) might have achieved, but it is likely that Jack Kennedy, the 35th President of the United States, pursued his political career because of his father's need to be President, rather than his own.

Because we need and want our parents' approval, we will fulfill any (expressed or assumed) role that our parent needs us to fulfill. I emphasize the word *need* because it may be very different from what the parents' consciously *say* they *want* for the child. If our childhood period of attachment is determined by our parents' needs, rather than our own, then our attachment will be prolonged beyond what is healthy for us.

I often see clients who have been taught that they need to share their feelings with their children. They call it "being honest with their kids." Unfortunately, this "tell all" kind of sharing satisfies parental needs *at the expense* of the child.

Too often parents restate, or try to "correct" a child's feelings, especially if the feelings are not to the liking of the parent. For example:

Child: *"I hate you, Mommy."*

Mother: *"You don't hate Mommy, you love Mommy."* Or,

"It hurts Mommy when you say that." Or,

"Then Mommy hates you too."

Those messages imply that our feelings are wrong, that our feelings cause their pain, and that it is not safe to express our feelings.

Appropriate, healthy responses to the child's expressed feeling of "I hate you, Mommy" could be:

"You are feeling very angry right now." Or,

"You are feeling pretty strong about this aren't you?" Or,

"I'm glad that you are telling me how you feel. Sometimes it is hard to find out what those feelings are--good for you!" Or,

"I can see you are having lots of feelings about this. Can you tell me more about them so we can clear the air?"

The appropriate message for us to receive, as children, should be that our feelings are expressions of our own internal experiences, and they should not devastate our parents or change the existing relationship with them. Instead, our feelings should be encouraged and validated.

As we grow up, expressing our feelings permits us to become separate from our parents. We then can feel safe being a person with separate feelings, separate decisions, and a separate self. Only after achieving this separateness will we be able to relate as an adult to our parents and to the world at large.

Parents may think or feel or say, "My kids should appreciate all I have done for them. When do I get my thanks from them? Is it all give?" The short answer to these ponderings is that it *is* all give until the child is separate.

True appreciation cannot be given by an "underling," someone who is beholden to the giver. The definition of appreciation can emphasize this point: To appreciate is to "estimate the quality, value, significance, or magnitude of;

To be fully *aware* of or sensitive to; realize." [101] We cannot know the meaning or value of a parent's efforts until we are an individuated adult.

Focusing on my parents playing with my toys is most important!

WHEN WE MUST FOCUS ON OUR PARENTS' NEEDS
Role Reversal

There is a difference between needing a child for gratification and being a needy parent. When a parent looks to us to tend their needs and take care of him or her is the third way that prevents us from becoming our own persons.

Relatedness is essential to development. We develop according to our experience of ourselves in relationship to others. As we interact, we form beliefs about how relationships work, and these beliefs form our future reality about how we will relate to others. It is in the process of everyday life that we experience developmental relationships--with positive or negative outcomes. In order to grow, we need an environment of empathy.

Once we realize that our feelings, ideas, or behavior can affect our parents' well-being, we experience what is called a *role reversal*. When we learn that we have the ability to hurt or not hurt our parents, we decide that we will take care of them. We do this because we feel we will receive love if we do. Unfortunately, role reversal happens all too often. Once we become attached as the caretaker of our parents, we attach forever, because separation would mean abandoning our parents who were (and continue to be) unable to take care of their own feelings. In this subtle and unconscious way, we become sacrifices to our parents and never become our own persons. We sacrifice our individuality to make our parents happy. We feel as though we are bad when we are being who we are, and when we make our parents unhappy.

If you're thinking, "What is wrong with that?" I suggest that there is *lots wrong with that*. The first problem is that it is impossible to "make someone else happy." The expectation that we can make a parent happy is one of an overwhelming burden.

Barry Neil Kaufman describes the frustration we might express when we feel bad when we fail to make our parents happy. A child may cry out in frustration:

> "Hey, I didn't ask to be born." My very existence is a cause of pain and suffering. I now listen carefully and very cautiously so I will know what to do because I now *believe* what I want is bad. My parent ties his/her self-worth to me.
>
> "If being me is bad, then I must learn to be not-me, which others say is good. Then, I have much self-doubt and insecurity about who I am. Since I want to be loved and since I want a peaceful environment, there must be something wrong with me if I generate dissonance in others. [102]

I believe that most parents do their very best to raise the children that God has given to them. I suppose that there are some bad parents but I have never met one. Every parent that I know wants what he or she believes is best for their child. The point is, that parents do not receive formal training to be a parent. There is no license to do the most important job in the world. People make mistakes.

Is it OK to do your best and have that best not be good enough? It is all that we know. Ignorance, however, *does not justify a defense*.

To climb the ladder of success is man's destiny.
To pass my father on this ladder is the climb to Mount Everest.

WHEN WE CANNOT SURPASS OUR PARENTS

The most devastating parents to have are those who are self-righteous and defensive. Defensive parents are constantly protecting their own fragile egos, and, thus, are in competition with us. If our parents are defensive parents, we learn early that we do not have permission to surpass them in any manner, because our parent will "feel bad" if we are perceived as "better." When we are not separated in a healthful manner, we feel we must continue to take care of our parent's fragile ego.

All too often competent men fail to succeed in business beyond the level of their fathers. They employ unconscious sabotages that cause them to stay below, or at least not above, a father's level of success. As time goes on, this type of sabotage is played out by a fear of success (fear of being more successful than our fathers) or by a fear of failure (fear that we cannot live up to our father's expectations.)

> Irv is a 40-year-old man who grew up poor because his father could not keep a job and continually got fired. Irv is intelligent and capable, but he cannot keep a job either. He gets good jobs and tires of them or quits them, and then remains out of work for long periods of time. He bought his own company, and at the height of its success, he sold it, making a huge profit. He then proceeded not to get another job and spend the profit on living expenses, until it was all gone. At one point he paid two "head hunters" large sums of money to locate a position for him. They didn't. He seemed to need to get rid of the money in order not to surpass his father.

Often I see people who begin college, but quit, lacking only one or a few credits before receiving their degree. These persons are often those whose parents never graduated from college. At the Ph.D. level, the phrase "ABDer's" is applied to graduate students who have done 4 years of course work and have all but the dissertation completed to get their doctorate.

223

Carl is an excellent tennis player who can not achieve a ranking higher than his tennis-playing father. Whenever he wins enough tournaments to exceed the highest ranking his father used to have, he loses the next several matches to players whom he should beat easily. As soon as his ranking drops, he defeats the same players easily.

WHEN WE CANNOT BE HAPPIER THAN OUR PARENTS

Another consequence of having a defensive parent, is that we cannot be happier than our parents.

Sally spent most of her teen and adult years on drugs. Her mother was a miserable, complaining, defensive woman who had abused Sally physically and emotionally all her years at home. At age 40, Sally stopped taking drugs and completely turned her life around but she could not seem to go any further. Although Sally had resolved much of the hurt about the abuse, she seemed stuck. To be happy meant complete abandonment of her mother--perhaps even her mother's death (in unconscious fantasy).

If our parents are in competition with us, then the unconscious message is that we cannot outdo them. If *they* are unhappy, then *we* must be unhappy. If *they* are unsuccessful, then *we* must be unsuccessful. If *they* are unable, then *we* must be unable as well.

Unhappiness is shown to be highly valued. "If you feel sad when I feel sad, then I feel better." "If you feel good when I am feeling bad, then I feel worse." The staging is precise. The beliefs are illustrated repeatedly, and concretely translated to us. [103]

This behavior is frequently obvious in children raised by parents in the military. Mary Edwards Wertsch, in her book *Military Brats, Legacies of*

Childhood Inside The Fortress, describe such a child's life:

> In the family, no matter where the warrior falls in the rank-conscious hierarchy of the military, the father is the general, the mother is the colonel, the older siblings are noncoms, and the youngest are the miserable new recruits. Like its larger military context, the family tends to have a very clear and generally inflexible chain of command. The virtue of this system must surely be its clarity. The person on each tier knows exactly what is expected and how far one can and cannot go...The down-side is role rigidity, which can be inhibiting to personal growth and can actually contribute to family conflict when the individuals resent their powerlessness to make opinions and feelings heard." [104]

The military roles are clearly defined. In some ways, this makes life easier, but it limits us to Stage Two, the rule-following stage of growth. In the typical, non-military family, roles are more subtly defined, but nonetheless as rigidly adhered to.

WHEN WE BECOME EMOTIONAL SURROGATE SPOUSES

If our parents are separated or divorced, it is not uncommon for one or more of the children to "take care of" the mother (or father, in some cases) by pleasing her or him.

We might make mom egg sandwiches, drink with her, stay up late watching TV with her, bring her flowers, tell her how pretty she looks, or notice a new dress--not because we notice the pretty dress, but because we know that mentioning her appearance brings her pleasure. When this behavior is rewarded and we notice her pleasure, then we become focused on *her* needs and not *our* own growing. We do not get to be "kids." We must become emotional surrogate spouses.

When parents cannot stand the competition, they might need to keep us incompetent. In this case, the parent, rewards only continuing childlike behavior. Any change in our childhood behavior is a threat.

225

Andy wrapped gifts in newspaper when he was a young child. Later in life, when he began wrapping gifts in regular wrapping paper, his parents seemed disappointed and would refer to the newspaper on each gift-giving occasion. Andy felt obligated to wrap the next present in newspaper "like old times."

Bobby had difficulty with math in the sixth grade, and although he became very proficient in math as an adult, his parents treated him as if he were incapable of understanding business.

Tony had difficulty in school. He is now 27 years old and his father still sees him as "having difficulty" and sends him money "to help out." When an exceptional job opportunity was available in Tony's father's company, he never considered Tony as a possible candidate. When Tony asked him about the job, his father was startled that Tony even thought he was qualified--even though Tony excelled in the same type of job in another company.

HEALTHY ATTACHMENT
ALLOWS FOR SUCCESSFUL SEPARATION
Unhealthy, prolonged attachment does not!

Most of the personal and interpersonal problems people face are caused either by attachment issues or separation issues. They are intertwined. The greater the abuse, the greater the attachment. The greater the unhealthy attachment, the less likely it is that separation will take place.

We all have a deep, natural need to be approved by our parents. The normal time for this approval is during the first seven years of our lives. That is the time when we are mirrored and validated. When this doesn't happen, we are stuck with the life-long task of doing everything in our power to obtain that mirroring and validation.

If, when we are young, our feelings are not acceptable as *our feelings*, then we learn that having our own feelings do not please our parents. We begin

226

looking for our parents' reactions to specific situations, rather than asking ourselves how *we* feel about them. We begin monitoring what we feel, and worry only about whether or not what we feel will be OK with our parents. *Doing* becomes more important than *being*.

As children, we should not be made to feel responsible for adult feelings in any manner. If we sense that our exploration, curiosity, uncertainties, and other emotions are not supported because they make our parents unhappy, then our developmental tasks will not be negotiated with a positive outcome. (See Table 1) The result is mistrust, guilt, shame, and doubt about who we are. When our behavior makes our parents unhappy, we feel directly responsible. Making our parents unhappy will continue to be totally unacceptable to us.

If we are not attached in a healthy way, we cannot achieve positive outcomes. (See Table 1) We continue to seek that attachment (the approval) for the rest of our lives. If we attach as we should, without the interference of parental needs, the next task is healthy separation.

Without successful separation, we are disabled. We need to identify and resolve the old beliefs and behaviors. Then we can live well in the present.

Before separation can begin we need to know what it is that we are attached to, and what form it takes.

Are we attached to being good, so that we can finally get approval?

Are we locked into what is familiar?

No matter what we do, do we continue to be abused or ignored?

We need to know our attachment, what it is that we are enmeshed in, before we can begin the adventure of separation.

When a client comes into therapy, I ask what event prompted him or her to call to me. That event often represents a kernel of the most important work that needs to be done. The event usually points to an awareness of a dysfunctional pattern in the client's life. The awareness causes pain or anxiety.

Kate told me she found herself in the middle of a chain store grocery instead of the exclusive, expensive market she usually patronized, because she needed to avoid her friends. The dysfunctional pattern was that "appearances were everything".

A couple began therapy after one of their frequent fights had been heard by the neighbors, through a window inadvertently left open. Their dysfunctional pattern was that "fighting is OK as long as it is kept a secret".

Attachment, in an average expectable environment, is essential for growth. Being attached and taken care of properly is the basis for normal living. Prolonged attachment is harmful. A bell didn't ring alerting us to when separation should have begun. So, as adults we need to be aware of destructive patterns developed early in our lives.

Many times we marry someone with our parents' exact traits, in an unconscious effort to resolve issues with them. For example, adult children of alcoholic parents frequently marry alcoholics with the hope that they will be able to change their spouse, in a way that they could not change their parents.

Howard, whose case was discussed earlier, is the fourth of eight children. His father was alcoholic. Howard had been given little attention as a child, and spent most of his teen-age years feeling depressed. Howard remembers helping his older brother hide liquor so that their father would not get drunk. The father died at age 54 and Howard never forgave himself for not being able to save him. Howard married an alcoholic. When she attempted suicide, he brought her into therapy to be "fixed". He was willing to help himself as long as the end result was that she was "fixed". When I told him that he could not "fix" her, he was visibly upset. He would not believe this. He said, "I feel driven to change her. I have to."

The issue here is not changing her. It is Howard's deep attachment to his father, from whom he had not separated. His wife's problem is only incidental to his original "attachment/never separated" story.

Joan is the oldest of five siblings. Her parents were both only children, and although they were educated and responsible parents, they were unaffectionate, unavailable and uninvolved with the children. Joan was given less than the other children because she demanded less attention by being "good" and taking care of herself. Even today, her mother, who lives nearby, never visits Joan, but drives to see her sisters who live farther away. The mother's reason is "they aren't doing as well as Joan." Joan is a successful lawyer who is ignored by her partner in the firm. She continues to be "good," demanding little and taking care of herself. What brought her into therapy was her frustration at the way the partner was treating her. The issue was not being ignored by him, but rather an unresolved issue with her parents, from whom she has not separated. Her partner is incidental to the original "attachment/never separated" story.

When a psychodynamic issue is described, and we become aware of what we are doing to ourselves, we often respond with disbelief. We cannot conceive that there is any connection. When we discover that our parents weren't perfect parents, or that our behavior is still tied to them in some way, we immediately defend them. Howard said, "He *did* provide for all of us." Joan said, "Although she didn't give me her opinion on anything, she *did have* a great sense of humor." When we need to defend our parents, it is possible that we are repeating a pattern that began with them, and we can be fairly sure we are still attached.

Allyson is the second of four children. Her father was an abusive man who was verbally cruel and physically absent from the family. Her parents divorced when she was seven, and her father ignored her from that day forward. She invites him to her family events with her husband and two daughters. Her father says that he will come, but does not show up, and never calls to say he isn't coming. Allyson first married a pathological liar, the father of her daughters. She came to see me when her second husband, of less than a year, began abusing her verbally and threatened to kill himself. Allyson married her "father" twice!

Resolution of unresolved issues with our parents is essential for *separation* and *individuation*. It is important for issues to be clarified and resolved. It is also important that we forgive our parents, but not until we have resolved our issues with them, which is the topic of the next chapter.

FORGIVING TOO SOON

"Heal the Past, Live the Present, Dream the Future"
—Bumper Sticker, 1993

Most of us believe or want to believe that our parents did the best they could. Despite our parents' limitations, we always seem to understand. Many therapists advocate forgiveness as essential to moving forward. I agree. The problem, is that if forgiveness is given *carte blanche* before the issues are recognized and responsibility assigned, we remain fixed in the belief system that caused the problems in the first place. We will continue to operate in that belief system over and over again, without any hope of altering the belief system or moving beyond it.

Forgiveness needs to take place at the end of the process of assigning responsibility, *not at the beginning*. Otherwise, we remain shamed, and unresolved issues will be repeated and repeated. John Bradshaw states that until we give up the idealization of our parents, we cannot heal our wounded inner child. 105

NOT FORGIVING

Unfortunately, we usually defend against resolving the issues with our parents, and "let them off the hook." If we don't defend our parents, we feel like we are betraying them. We remain in our old belief systems by subscribing to the rationalizations that:

☐ "It is all in the past."

☐ "It will only make me hurt more."

☐ "It's better to forgive and forget."

☐ "He/she is too old now. Why hurt them?"

☐ "My parents did their best."

☐ "If I express my rage, they won't love me."

☐ "My childhood was fine."

☐ "It is too late now. I'm fine."

☐ "I've forgiven them long ago."

☐ "They couldn't handle it." [106]

ESSENTIAL FORGIVING

Louise Hay, in her book *Power is Within*, makes a point that forgiveness of our parents is essential to the forgiveness of ourselves. If we do not forgive them, we will tend to repeat the same damage to ourselves and our own children that our parents did to us as children. When we are mistreated as children, we do not have options. When we are adults, as long as we do not resolve those traumas, we continue to traumatize ourselves. It is all we know how to do. 107

If, on the other hand, we forgive our parents too soon, then we continue to assume that it was we who were to blame.

Forgiving, in and of itself, does not make lasting changes. It only puts off dealing with issues that are so painful they may not even exist in our consciousness.

Susan Forward, in her book *Toxic Parents*, says,

"There are two faces of forgiveness: giving up the need for revenge, and absolving the guilty party of responsibility. I felt there was something wrong with unquestioningly absolving someone of his rightful responsibility, particularly if he had severely mistreated an innocent child. Why would you pardon a father who terrorized and battered you, who made your childhood a living hell?...Forgiveness and absolution (without resolution) is really another form of denial....One of the dangerous things about forgiveness is that it undercuts your ability to let go of your pent-up emotions. How can you acknowledge your anger against a parent whom you've already forgiven? Responsibility can go only one of two places: outward, onto the people who have hurt you, or inward, into yourself. Someone's got to be responsible. So you may forgive your parents but end up hating yourself all the more in exchange." 108

PERCEPTIONS OF HURT

It is important to emphasize that what happens to us has as much to do with our perceptions of what happened, as with what actually happened. We must confront these perceptions. The best-intentioned parents operate on the knowledge imparted to them by their own parents, and their own perceptions of parenting.

One client's mother sent him to his room when he came home late from school. He was not traumatized because his parents had already set boundaries, and consequences. In a similar situation, another adult client remembers feeling abandoned and unloved.

"Look son, your mother and I held the fort all day.
Take your ball and go to your room."

It is not up to our parent to decide our perception. What is important, is for our parent to assume the responsibility for sending us to our room. If that act was hurtful to us, our parent needs to acknowledge the act and the way we perceived it. If the perception was one of hurt, our parent can apologize for his part in our feeling hurt. The intention of our parent and our perception can be different. It is a rarely the intention of any parent to hurt us. Hurt, however, is our reality. Our perception of being hurt must be dealt with in order to resolve our issues. When we have resolved our issues, then, and only then, are we in a position to "forgive" our parent. Without identifying our issues, confronting those involved, and resolving the issues, we cannot separate. We remain disabled. To live well in the present, we must clear out the unresolved problems in the past.

After resolution is accomplished, forgiveness is necessary and successful separation possible. Successful separation is the subject of the next chapter.

SUCCESSFUL SEPARATION

"Until one is committed, there is hesitancy, the chance to draw back, always ineffectiveness. Concerning all acts of initiative (and creation), there is one elementary truth, the ignorance of which kills countless ideas and splendid plans; that the moment one definitely commits oneself, then Providence moves too. All sorts of things occur to help one that would never otherwise have occurred. A whole stream of events issues from the decision, raining in one's favour all manner of unforeseen incidents and meetings and material assistance, which no man could have dreamed would have come his way."
—W. H. Murray

Once we decide to separate and face the unresolved issues with our parents, our journey begins. Susan Forward, in her book *Toxic Parents*, gives a good outline for resolving such issues.

1. State what happened.

2. State how we felt about what happened at the time.

3. State how it has affected our life today.

4. State what needs to be done now. 109

The process of closure with past events requires only that all the appreciations and resentments be clearly stated.

The journey is not easy. We might get discouraged in trying to "buck City Hall." To achieve closure we may make waves. It is telling the emperor he has no clothes. Closure is tough business. We fantasize that it is too late, that it doesn't matter any more, that our parents couldn't handle it, that it might kill them or that we would lose (or never get) the love we have worked so many years to earn.

REALIZING THE NECESSITY OF SEPARATION

The moment of *realizing* that separation is necessary may *feel like a death*. When we are separated and reborn into being our own person, we will be tested. The tests occur when we choose a different type of man (unencumbered by the past unresolved issues), or a different job with a boss who respects us (unlike the father who abused us)., It may be that the new situation feels unfamiliar, uncomfortable, even boring. The realization that we need to lay new groundwork for our new identity is a crisis that will need to be weathered.

Frances' father died before she was born. Her mother raised her alone and was eccentric, unreliable and verbally abusive all during Frances's life. Frances had a series of relationships with men who were equally abusive and whom she could not rely. Her last boyfriend stole money from her, hocked her rings to buy alcohol, and, in a violent rage, smashed a bay window that cost Frances $800 to repair. After completing therapy she met a man who was reliable, stable, kind, responsible, and who loved her and wanted to marry her. She continued to be surprised when he kept his agreements and when he came home when he said he would be home, and discussed problems unemotionally. Frances had to get used to being treated in an normal, expectable way.

238

Benny has anxiety about leaving home and separating from his mother. "It feels like the grim reaper will get me."

INDEPENDENCE VS. ATTACHMENT

We must be clear about what happened to us as a result of the extended attachment. We must remind ourselves how the failure to separate successfully has effected our lives, so that old patterns do not creep back in. We need to experience independence longer than we experienced attachment in order for the new behavior to be automatic.

We hang on to limiting relationships and a lower level of functioning, because *we know* what is coming next. The outcome is predictable. Living in the present is going beyond the known. To live as our own person means we will not know what is coming next. It will be uncomfortable and it may take practice not to panic--knowing that the future is truly a blank space in time. We have to be ready for new, unfamiliar behavior.

> The Christian Bible records that darkness followed the crucifixion of Christ. The darkness felt like a blank space in time because after Jesus died on the cross on Friday, all hope seemed gone. Believers in Jesus' death thought the end had come, unless God, indeed, could raise Him from the dead as was predicted. Without the story of the Resurrection, there would be no Christianity.

Without our separation, there is no individuated self-in-process

We were unintentionally manipulated into our unhealthy attachments by our parents, siblings, and other care-givers. We were shaped by their needs, expectations, good intentions, meanness, and ignorance. We survived but we remain constantly vigilant, so we will not be annihilated, unloved, or lose what minimal love we have. We remain attached to this quest for approval and survival.

Separation, and only separation, is the key to our individuation so we must be willing to experience the discomfort, that blank space. It is a struggle.

Successful separation requires *awareness,* and *introspection,* and *action.* Successful separation requires us to release our defense mechanisms so that we can "check-out" our reactive, automatic behaviors. We must begin to trust so that our self-in-process can experience life to its fullest. It is possible. It is up to each of us personally. It is our responsibility.

CONCLUSION: IT IS YOUR RESPONSIBILITY

"I think these difficult times have helped me
to understand better than before
how infinitely rich and beautiful life is
in every way and that so many things
that one goes around worrying about
are of no importance whatsoever."
—Isak Dinesen

We are swallowed up only when
we are willing for it to happen.
—Nathalie Sarraute

"The extent to which we love ourselves determines whether
we eat right, get enough sleep, smoke, wear seat belts,
exercise and so on. Each of these choices controls
about 90% of the factors that determine our state of health."
—Bernie Siegel

"The secret in life is to carry the enthusiasm of
childhood into adult life."
—Adolf Huxley

"On with the dance.
Let the joy be unconfined."
—Mark Twain

Allow me to summarize briefly.

When we are born, we are given a set of circumstances over which we have no control. Some of us get a good-enough mother and an average expectable environment. Some of us do not. We develop ways to survive. We develop belief systems about those perceptions and live a life within those belief systems. The way we are related to within those belief systems, determines the way we operate in the world. In order to feel accepted in life, we develop defense mechanisms to protect ourselves from hurts and disappointments.

BECOMING THE SELF-IN-PROCESS

We develop in a positive or negative way depending on how our developmental tasks are completed. Our level of attachment determines how attached we remain. For our true self-in-process to emerge, we must overcome the ego defense mechanisms and transcend our egos. In order to do this, we must separate from the dependence that keeps us from actualizing our potential.

Separation begins with assigning responsibility to ourselves or to others for what really happened for us. We must identify, re-experience, and grieve past losses and traumas in order to clearly work though basic belief systems that are no longer useful.

Once responsibility is assigned and resolution is accomplished, we can shed the past and accept responsibility for who we are now as individuals. As individuals we can identify our needs and learn how to get them met.

In many instances, we were victims. In many instances we took the easy way out. Whatever the case, *it is now our responsibility to move forward*. Hanging on to the past in order to justify the present is self-defeating. Needing to continue to believe what we believed in the past is as archaic as using a horse and buggy for transportation or a carrier pigeon as the only means of communication. Times change, and we must adapt to the change by looking at what we are doing. No one else can look at where we have been. No one else can get a handle on our defense systems. Only we can do it. If we rely on "That's the way I am" as an excuse, we will remain stuck. On the other hand, we can ask ourselves:

"What belief keeps me the way I am?"

"Why do I continue behavior that does not serve me well?"

"When will I be separate from past issues so that I can be at choice?"

AWARENESS IS THE KEY

Awareness is the key to choice. Becoming aware of our limiting or self-defeating belief systems is the only way we can begin to make real choices about our lives. Without awareness there are no choices. We can begin to be aware of where we are by numerous means. Recognizing where we are on the continuum of growth, or finding our what roles we play, are two good ways of becoming aware. It is necessary to risk anxiety and grieve in order to individuate.

On my check-out dive for certification as a scuba diver, I was first to enthusiastically jump into the water. I found myself bobbing around in the ocean with instructions to dive down and wait on the bottom of the ocean floor 30 feet below the surface. I put my regulator in my mouth and it felt like I couldn't get any air. The more I tried to draw air, the more anxiety I felt. The instructor repeatedly yelled from the boat, "Alice, put your head in the water."

I was trying to apply old principles to a new situation. I forgot that the regulator is constructed to enable me to breathe under the water, not on top! I was trying to feel comfortable with old ways before

243

putting my head in the water and certifying myself for a new adventure. Trust me, I know how difficult it is to give up the old ways.

WHAT WE CAN DO TO PROCEED

Put your head in the water! Prove you can *do something by doing something else.* Things get better by risk, not by chance. Limiting or self-defeating belief systems are a result of remaining attached or, worse yet, still longing to become attached to our parents. Resistance to the needed introspection leaves us in the shadow of chance. Rigidly holding on to what is past leaves us brittle and prevents our self from ever being "in process." Being rigid does not mean we are stable or secure. Increasing the alternatives to life's predicaments permits us more possibilities of choice and leaves less of life "up to chance".

If we can reach Stage Four and become responsible for our thoughts and actions, we can go on to create new choices, new habits and a more conscious life.

Consider the barriers that we must challenge to uncover these very deeply embedded core beliefs. They are indications that we have not yet separated:

- ☐ Co-dependence
- ☐ Defensiveness
- ☐ Procrastination
- ☐ Mistrust
- ☐ Low self-esteem
- ☐ Rigidity
- ☐ Time-incompetence
- ☐ Age-inappropriate dependency

- ☐ Addictions
- ☐ Shame
- ☐ Fear
- ☐ Arrogance
- ☐ Self-pity
- ☐ Stubborness
- ☐ Bad habits
- ☐ Acting out
- ☐ Acting in

To recognize that we are using these barriers to avoid change is the first step in digging out and confronting the core belief systems that keep us dependent on our past and from realizing our potential. 110

These barriers may *seem* overwhelming, but recognizing the barriers enables us to knock them down. Uncovering the core is like peeling an onion layer by layer. It takes time, it's not easy, but with patience, it is worth it!

The process of clearing away the barriers that prohibit us from resolving issues takes energy but so does maintaining the barriers. We can do anything we get excited about and put energy into. Why not put the energy into becoming fully individuated rather than holding back from moving forward?

Treat new information as a wonderful nugget that may be gold. Don't throw it away before examining it and appraising it. If it is gold, (that is, if it allows you to have an *awareness* you did not have before), you will be rich!

OK, WHAT ARE YOUR BELIEF SYSTEMS? CHALLENGING YOUR UNCONSCIOUS

HOW TO HELP YOURSELF TO SELF-HELP

"What makes transition periods like a mid-life-crisis, problematic and painful is that in successfully working our way through them we must give up cherished notions, old ways of doing and looking at things."
—M. Scott Peck

"Do you love life?
Then, do not squander time
for that's what life is made of."
—Benjamin Franklin

"If it's to be, it's up to me.
Refuse to make excuses for not making progress.
Refuse to rationalize. Refuse to justify.
Accept total responsibility.
Become totally self-reliant."
—Brian Tracy

Throughout this book, we have considered the belief systems and the questions that must be asked to discover them:

What are my belief systems?

What triggered them in the first place?

Why did I react the way I did?

What meaning did I give these happenings?

What defenses did I build to protect myself from harm?

When am I defensive?

Am I procrastinating? Why am I procrastinating?

How are those belief systems controlling me now?

Are my old reactions still appropriate? Am I on automatic?

The answers to these questions challenge your unconscious. The answers may make you uncomfortable.

In the case histories described, we saw that some people choose to change their belief systems--and their lives. Others would not, or could not tolerate the "emotional discomfort" of change.

Your interest in this book, indicates that you desire change--that you are willing and ready to make changes, to move forward, unload, and stop getting in your own way. If you feel this way, you are in, at least, Stage Three, the truth-seeking stage of growth in process.

WHERE DO YOU BEGIN?

This final chapter describes how to challenge your unconscious and locate your beliefs. It also provides practical methods for examining them.

THE FRAMING OF BELIEF SYSTEMS

Imagine that each one of your belief systems is contained within its own picture frame. Some frames contain beliefs about a parent, a spouse, a boyfriend or child. Some frames enclose beliefs about how well you do in your job, or play a sport, or perform as a sexual partner. You will discover many frames holding beliefs about your image. One might focus on beliefs about how you look--beliefs that limit your enjoyment of social activities, dating or marriage.

"Frame," (the noun), is defined as "something composed of parts, fitted and joined together." You have placed each one of your belief systems in a frame of your own choosing. That frame surrounds and limits all the data about a particular belief. Consciously or unconsciously, you have chosen what to put *inside* the frame--and what to leave *out*.

If you were to display all your "framed" belief systems, they might fit on your desk top. They might cover all of the walls of one room, or all the walls in your home. Together, they form your personal frame of reference.

"Frame of reference" is defined as "a set or system of ideas (as in philosophical or religions doctrine) in which other ideas are interpreted or assigned meaning." Psychologically, your framed belief systems provide a frame of reference which includes all your (recognizable and hidden) memories, happenings, thoughts, hopes, emotions, reasons, actions, reactions-- from childhood to present.

To examine your entire frame of reference at once would be overwhelming! But you can begin by examining your belief systems--one at a time--when you notice how you have framed them.

249

> I perceived my body to be huge, because my mother said that this
> outfit or that dress "made me look too big." I believed my mother's
> opinion about my size. I also believed my mother's comments that "I was
> ugly." I put various pieces of data together, and placed a frame around
> my mother's negative (and untrue) perceptions--which, for many years,
> I carried as a powerful, painful, and negative false belief system about
> my body.

The illustration above shows how a belief system may be constructed. I lived
with these beliefs about my body for a long time. Only later in life, was I able
to identify them as destructive and false parts of my frame of reference.

HOW TO REFRAME YOUR BELIEF SYSTEMS

To *Reframe* (as a verb) does not exist as a single word in most commonly-
used dictionaries, or nor in psychological dictionaries. But the prefix, *Re*, does
help describe the process of "reframing" our belief systems. The prefix "Re"
adds the concepts of "again," "back again," "against," and "backwards" to
words that it modifies. It also can mean "*recall*" (as in look backwards) and
"*retell*" (as in describe anew).

Notice that some of your framed belief systems are placed in large
(important) frames. Other frames are tiny (and seemingly insignificant). Some
pictures are beautifully matted and mounted in expensive frames. Other
pictures are time-worn and dusty. The images inside a few frames are so small,
so faint or crowded, that the picture is blurred and confusing.

You react differently to each picture. You may feel happy, proud or
motivated by some. You may feel sad, embarrassed, discouraged, angry,
disturbed or upset about others. You enjoy looking at your favorite pictures.
You have placed others face down, so you won't have to look at them. Still
others may be "forgotten"--"lost" and buried deep in drawers or closets.

We can visualize the process of framing (or reframing) a painting, photo or
document. Selecting the frame is not easy. The frame must complement and
"fit" the subject (belief system). Choosing the "right" frame requires decisions

(perceptions and judgements) about size, color, feeling, shape, finish and cost.

Once that picture has been framed, it reflects a part of our interests (our frame of reference), and once hung in our house (our life), it is not likely to be framed again for a long time. It might be reframed if we redecorated our entire house (changing our frame of reference), or if the picture began a new life--in a new location, with a new owner (the you, who is changing your life view).

When you recognize a belief system that may be destructive or bothersome, you can study that picture to find out why those particular beliefs came to be. You can find out how they are still affecting your life. Then, you can change your perception of those beliefs--and *reframe* that belief system.

> When I was at Esalen studying Gestalt Therapy with Jim Simkin, our cook for the workshop was a woman five feet, nine inches tall (my height) who weighed, I would guess, around 250 pounds. She was very comfortable with her body. In fact, she was a professional model who was booked years in advance. She was then also president of the American Models Association.
>
> She and I talked about our body images. I, who was 5'9'' and weighed 132 pounds, felt huge and uncomfortable in my body. She who was the same height and weighed almost twice as much as I, felt (and was) beautiful and very comfortable in her body. The difference in our attitudes came from very different frames of reference.

The *facts* of my belief system remained the same. I was tall, but not everyone believed that I was too tall, or that by being tall, I was also ugly. I was the one who framed those beliefs.

Obtaining new insight about an old belief system, allowed me to consider re-framing it with a new frame.

After talking with the tall woman at Esalen, my frame of reference for "huge" was altered--not only in terms of weight and size, but in terms of a positive attitude toward my body. My concepts of big or small were changed. My concept of big or large as synonymous with bad or ugly was changed. My size, big or small, had nothing to do with beautiful or ugly. The chance meeting at Esalen provided me with a liberating "Ah Ha!" While nothing about me changed physically, I had re-framed the belief system about my body image and I now saw myself as a medium-sized, a positive, slender, attractive woman.

The same result could *not* have been achieved by "positive thinking." Positive thinking and the use of affirmations can help us keep a healthy focus on life. However, the transformation (reframing) of my belief system required the action of choice--which is much different from just thinking positively about a negative situation. When you find yourself using the words "challenge" or "opportunity" in place of "problem" you may be placing yourself in denial and trying to rise above the issue instead of dealing with its resolution.

I had been willing to acknowledge the problem, I noticed a clue that led me to consider an alternate possibility. Acting on those insights, I was able to reframe my old belief, with a new frame--the kind of frame that surrounds a happy, liberating belief, seen in a new light.

PHYSICAL CLUES ABOUT BELIEF SYSTEMS

The last pages of this book provide suggestions for specific ways to discover, observe and change old belief systems. One commonly-overlooked clue is the way in which our physical bodies react, as my following experience illustrates.

My husband, Kim, and I played mixed doubles in tennis tournaments since 1976. We won lots of tournaments, which enabled us to play the Family Challenge at the U.S. Open where we reached the semi-finals. In 1989 Kim won the National Indoors Men's Doubles title, and our local tournament committee rated him a notch above me in the division in which we competed as a team.

We continued to compete in the higher division, but were no longer as competitive. We lost in the first or second rounds, instead of somewhat regularly reaching the semi-final or final rounds. I suddenly developed a severe knee injury. I could no longer drive a car without an automatic transmission or walk up stairs without pain. Obviously, tennis was out of the question.

Over a six month period I consulted chiropractors, orthopedic surgeons, and acupuncturists. There were a variety of diagnoses and prescriptions, but the pain did not subside. Then one day, when I was reading *Heal Your Body,* I looked up knee problems. The probable emotional cause of knee problems suggested is: "Stubborn ego and pride. Inability to bend. Fear. Inflexibility. Won't give in." [110]

I was startled. It all made sense. The affirmation and new thought pattern connected with a knee injury is: "Forgiveness. Understanding. Compassion. I bend and flow with ease, and all is well."

I had been angry with the committee for putting Kim in a rating category higher than mine. My ego and pride couldn't manage that fact that he was better than I, and my knee problem allowed me an excuse to not face it.

Once I saw that reality, my knee problem ceased and I have not experienced any pain since. The pain in my knee allowed my ego to protect me from facing the fact that I would not play competitively with Kim again. I could accept that decision based on those facts, without becoming crippled.

All the positive thinking in the world would not have fixed my knee, because my need to be injured served a greater purpose. I had to see that what I was doing to myself was ridiculous. I needed to see that my emotion (my ego) was preventing me from moving forward into another phase of my life (self-in-process). The cause of my injury, my dis-ease, had to be confronted and resolved.

Now, when clients arrive for a therapy session with an ache, pain, or injury, I frequently consult Louise Hays' book, *Heal Your Body* or Wayne Topping's book *What Makes You Sick Makes You Tick* [111] to look for a possible emotional cause of the discomfort. The relationship of thoughts and emotions to our physical body may elude us. But, physical problems do make us sit up and pay attention. Physical reactions can lead us to important truths, as the incident described.

"Joe uses his construction skills to reframe his outlook on life."

PREPARING FOR CHANGE

We become ready for change by studying the belief systems in our frame of reference. We change by re-framing the beliefs about the "self" we used to be.

Beneath the following topics are listed questions you have a right to ask yourself. They can jog your memory and heighten your awareness. The answers will be important. When you find the answers, you will discover belief systems that govern your thoughts, feelings and actions today.

Look back into your childhood...

What are your first memories? What does it mean when you remember these happenings back in time?

Ask your parents what they remember about you as a child.

What are the "funny stories" that are repeated about you as part of the family lore?

Describe the family roles...

What role did you play in your family of origin?--The clown? The counselor? The peace-maker? The scapegoat?

Was there an "identified patient" or problem in your family? What was the purpose of having someone "sick" or "bad"?

What were the invisible loyalties? Is it OK for you to be better-- happier, more successful, richer, more sexual, more educated than your parents or other family members? Is it (was it) OK to have your own needs when those needs seemed to be in conflict with family myths?

Who was defensive?

Who or what was being protected?

What were the verbal and non-verbal messages of your family?

What are your family myths? ("No one in our family gets divorced." "The man in the family wears the pants." "Be nice,

255

everyone likes our family.")

What were and are the secrets in your family?

What are the power struggles in your family?

Is there triangulation in your relationships?
Who forms the triangles? What purpose does the triangle serve?
Who is being protected?

Was there score keeping?

What were the unwritten rules your family lived by?

Evaluate how your family communicated...

Was your family open, closed, directionless?

Did family members send clear, honest, direct messages?
If not, why?

Was it clear which behavior was optional, preferential, required?

Describe how you reason or think now...

To what are you entitled? Why?

What are your prejudices?
Whose were they before they were yours?

What do your think is unfair? Why?

Examine your emotions...

What makes you angry?

What makes you feel guilty?

What makes you feel shame?

What makes you laugh?

What causes you to cry in a movie, in a play, or when you hear certain music or sounds? What's behind the tears?

Notice your strongest interests...

Who are your heroes now, and who were your heroes in the past? Why were they your heroes?

Whom do your admire? Why?

What books do you read? Why?

What do you watch on TV? Why?

To what are you committed?

Describe your behaviors, relationships and attitudes...

What do you dislike (and like) in yourself most? Why?

To whom are you committed?

Whom do you see as friends?

Is honest feedback encouraged (allowed) in your circle of friends, family?

What about your family still embarrasses you? Why?

What are the unwritten rules you now live by?

What do you lie about? Why?

When do you exaggerate? About what?
What does it make better?

If you are addicted to something, what is it?
Why are you addicted to that? What rewards come from that addiction? What thoughts of actions do you associate with that addiction? ("I need a drink to relax." "If I'm thin, I will be popular.")

If a certain answer seems obvious, ask what would happen if the answer was different? If you feel you are right and need to be right, ask, "Why?"-- and ask what is behind that need.

Monitor your behaviors...

First and foremost, ask yourself why you need to defend yourself. What belief system are you defending?
Does that belief system or defense apply now?

When you procrastinate, ask "What as I avoiding?" "Why?"
If you are late, look behind the reason.
Why do you think you were late?

If you are resistant, angry or hurt, don't hide behind unresolved issues--or claim your feelings are someone else's fault. Find out what is behind issues you don't want to face.

Be alert to patterns in your life. When a situation occurs once, it is a "happening," but if the same incident or action re-occurs, it may indicate a "pattern." Then, ask yourself,
"What is going on here that is unresolved?"

"Sayings" you grew up with may reveal more about your belief systems. Write down the ones you remember. "Early to bed and early to rise makes a man healthy, wealthy and wise" and "A penny saved is a penny earned" are good examples.

GAIN INSIGHT FROM YOUR DAILY ROUTINES

You can find out the difference between your myths and your reality by examining what in life is important to you. Look at your *behavior,* not your *words.*

Make a list, with the endeavor, person or activity you feel is most important at the top. Keep a log of how you spend your days, hour by hour. At the end of a week, total the number of hours spent on each activity. Compare the results with your list of values. If the greatest number of hours recorded were *not* spent doing what you think you value most, ask, "Why?" Then, consider that the largest number of hours may represent what you *really value.*

Another approach to gaining insight, is to list the three things you most like to do, and the three things you least like to do. Discover what belief system established those preferences.

259

Fill in the personality and preference quizzes that appear in magazines and books. Notice what insights the results may provide. You don't have to "swallow" all the ideas, just "consider" them.

Keep a journal. Record the belief systems you discover. Keep a record of how your life changes as a result of your discoveries.

YOUR PERSONAL POWER

Now that you understand more about belief systems and how they become your frame of reference, you can begin to reframe your pictures--and your life.

If something is holding you back in life, find the limiting or self-defeating belief system that causes the blockage. Resolve it! Be *at choice*. Growing may not be an easy task, but you are worth every bit of your effort. Your personal power depends on it.

You are the key. Your introspection and awareness are the missing links to improving your self-in-process. The quality of your present depends on how aware you are *in the here and now*. And the quality of your future can be shaped by your continued curiosity and willingness to see what there is out there for you, unencumbered by your past or other people's limitations or best intentions.

Best wishes on your journey
And blessings...

"Go confidently in the direction of your dream.
Act as if it is impossible to fail."
—Henry Thoreau

NOTES

Introduction

1. Erik Erikson. **Childhood and Society.** (New York: Norton, 1950), 247-274.

2. Bruce Dewe. "Sabotage Programmes" **Professional Health Provider Manual III**. 1990 (Switzerland: International Kinesiology College).

3. Gordon Stokes and Daniel Whiteside. **Structural Neurology.** (Burbank, California: Three In One Concepts Publications, 1989).

4. Erikson, 273.

Chapter 1

5. Wayne Dyer. **Real Magic**. Nightingale-Conant Corporation Tape Series, 1992.

6. Paula Oleska, "Emotional Integration," **Touch For Health Journal** 1992.

7. M. Scott Peck, **The Road Less Travelled** (New York: Simon & Schuster, 1978).

8. Wayne Topping, **What Makes You Tick, Makes You Sick** (Bellingham, Washington: Topping International Institute, 1992).

9. Jeffery Pease, "Exercising Your Emotional Options," **Body, Mind & Spirit** (March/April, 1993).

10. Frederick Perls, Lecture at Esalen Institute, 1969.

11. Lynn O. O'Conner, "Control Mastery Theory and Treatment of the Addict," **California Psychologist** (January 1993).

Chapter 2

12. Louise Hay, **Heal Your Body** (Carson, California: Hay House, Inc., 1984), 22.

13. Nancy Joekel, "The Question of Choice," (paper presented at the Touch For Health Annual Meeting, 1978).

14. Abraham Maslow, **Toward A Psychology of Being** (Princeton, New Jersey. Van Nostrand, 1968). Later in Maslow's life he postulated that there were needs even beyond those of self-actualization. He stated that the highest needs were self-transcendence, a spiritual attainment in which we have a need to be involved with something that transcends our own life, something that gives us immortality, a legacy and a meaning.

15. Harold F. Searles, **My Work With Borderline Patients** (Northvale, NJ: Jason Aronson: 1986), 217.

16. John Bradshaw, **On Homecoming Series**, Public Broadcasting System, 1990.

17. Ellen Bass and Laura Davis, **Courage To Heal** (New York: Harper & Row. 1989).

Chapter 3

18. Erikson, Erik **Identity, Youth and Crisis** (New York: W.W. Norton & Co. Inc. 1968).

19. D.W. Winnicott. Arthur Kovacs class notes. California School of Professional Psychology, Los Angeles, 1979.

20. William Glasser, **Reality Therapy** (New York: Harper & Row, 1965).

21. Rollo May, **Freedom and Destiny** (New York: Norton, 1981).

22. Victor Frankl, **Man's Search For Meaning** (New York: Washington Square Press, 1997).

23. Wayne Dyer, **You Have to Believe It To See It** To Believe It (Nightingale-Conant Tape Series, 1989).

24. Stewart Emery, **Actualizations: You Don't Have To Rehearse To Be Yourself** (New York: Doubleday & Company, Inc., 1978).

Chapter 4

25. Peck

26. Sir John Eccles, from Blair Justice, **Who Gets Sick** (Los Angeles. J.P. Tarcher, 1988), 15.

27. ibid, 16.

28. DeePak Chopra, Lecture at Church of Religious Science, Glendale 1992.

29. Wayne Dyer, **Real Magic** (Nightingale-Conant Tape Series: 1992).

30. Bradshaw.

31. A postscript: My mother read this book as a manuscript. She said she hadn't realized she had effected me in this way. As we talked more she told me she didn't think I was a pretty child. My belief system that she just did not want to toot her own horn was a rationalization that I used to justify not liking how she felt about my looks.

32. Ashley Montagu, **Elephant Man, A Study in Human Dignity** (New York: Ballantine Books, 1971).

Chapter 5

33. L.E. Hinsie and R.J. Campbell, **Psychiatric Dictionary,** (New York: Oxford University Press, 1960).

34. Henry Murray, in Alfred Freedman, Harold I. Kaplan and Benjamin J. Sadock, **Comprehensive Textbook of Psychiatry/I. Second Edition** (Baltimore: The Williams and Wilkins Company, 1975), 693.

35. Carl Jung, **Psychological Types.** (New York: Harcourt Brace, 1923).

36. Isabel Briggs Myers, **Introduction to Type** (Palo Alto, California: Consulting Psychologists Press, Inc., 1982).

37. David Keirsey and Marilyn Bates, **Please Understand Me** (Del Mar, California: Prometheus Nemesis Book Company, 1984).

38. Lynn Namka, **Doormat Syndrome**, Florida: Health Communications, Inc., 1989).

Chapter 6

39. Heintz Kohut, **The Search For The Self** (New York: International Universities Press, Inc., 1978).

40. Bradshaw

Chapter 7

41. Renee Spitz, In Freud, Anna. "Anaclitic Depression," **The Psychoanalytic Study of the Child**. Vol 2. Eds. Eissler, H. Freud, A. Hartman, H. Kris, E. New York: International Universities Press, 1942).

42. Jack Rosenberg, **Body, Self & Soul: Sustaining Integration** (Georgia: Humanics New Age, 1989), 19-20.

43. D.W. Winnicott, **Holding and Interpretation**. New York: Grove Press, 1972,1986), 20.

44. Robert Stolorow and George Atwood, **The Organizing Principle** (paper, 1992).

45. Michael Balient, **The Basic Fault** (London: Tavistock Publication: 1968), 59-73.

46. Margaret Mahler, **On Human Symbiosis and the Vicissitudes of Individuation** (New York: International Universities: 1968) on Rapproachment.

Chapter 8

47. Joe Luft and Harry Ingham, **The Johari Window, A Graphic Model for Interpersonal Relations** (Washington D.C.: Human Relations Training News: 1961).

48. Irving Yalom, **Theory and Practice of Group Psychotherapy**, (New York: Basic Books: 1975), 363.

49. Joe Luft, **Group Process**, (The National Press: 1963).

50. Matthew McKay, Martha David and Patrick Fannine, **Messages. The Communication Skills Book**, (Oakland, California: New Harbinger Publications, 1983), 31-35.

Chapter 9

51. Nancy Myer Hopkins, "Symbolic Church Fights," **Congregations**, (May-June, 1993).

52. William Morris, **American Heritage Dictionary** (Boston: Houghton Mifflin, 1982).

Chapter 10

53. Charles Whitfield **Healing the Child Within** Workshop handout, 1990.

54. Bruno Bettelheim, "Individual and Mass Behavior In Extreme Conditions." **Journal of Abnormal Social Psychology**. 1943, 38. 447-449.

55. Sigmund Freud, **Moses and Monotheism**, (London: Hogarth Press: 1939).

56. James C. Coleman, **Abnormal Psychology and Modern Life**, (Illinois: Scott, Foreman and Company: 1964), 104.

57. Steve Carter, **Men Who Can't Love, When A Man's Fear Makes Him Run From Commitment**, (New York: M. Evans and Co., 1987).

58. Coleman, 98.

59. Benjamin Franklin, Autobiography.

60. Coleman, 100.

61. Gerald H.J. Pearson, ed., **Handbook of Child Psychoanalysis** (New York: Basic Books, 1968).

62. Janette Rainwater, **You're In Charge** (Culver City, California: Peace Press, 1979).

63. Whitfield

Chapter 11

64. Joel Kovel, **A Complete Guide To Therapy** (New York: Pantheon Books, 1976), 262.

65.---"What is Co-Dependency?" (paper published by St. John's Hospital, Salina, KS).

66. Anne Wilson Schaef, **Co-Dependence: Misunderstood--Mistreated** (Cambridge: Harper & Row, 1986).

67. Morris

68. Emanuel E. Hammer, **The Use of Interpretation in Treatment**, (New York: Grune and Stratton, 1968), 303.

Chapter 12

69. McKay, 123.

70. Deepok Chopra, **Magical Mind, Magical Body** (Nightingale-Conant Tape Series: 1990).

71. Tom Gordon, **Parent Effectiveness Training** (New York: Peter H. Wyden, Inc, 1970).

72. Stephen Covey, **Applications of the Seven Habits of Highly Effective People** (Nightingale-Conant Tape Series, 1992).

Chapter 13

73. Morris, 217.

74. Whitfield

Chapter 14

75. **Webster's Dictionary of English Usage** (Springfield, Massachusetts: Merriam-Webster, 1989).

Chapter 15

77. Stewart Emery, **Actualizations: You Don't Have to Rehearse to Be Yourself** (New York: Doubleday & Company, Inc., 1978).

78. Whitfield

79. Shirley MacLaine, **Dance In The Light** (New York: Bantam Book, 1985), 18.

Chapter 16

80. Elisabeth Kubler-Ross, **On Death and Dying** (New York: Macmillan, 1969).

81. Gary Emery, **Own Your Own Life** (New York: New American Library, 1982).

82. Gordon Stokes and Daniel Whiteside, **Under The Code** (Burbank, California. Three In One Concepts Publication, 1985), 6-6.

83. M. Scott Peck **Further Along The Road Less Travelled** (Nightingale-Conant Tape Series, 1992)

84. Carl Rogers **On Becoming A Person** (Boston: Houghton Mifflin Company, 1961), 132.

85. Peck, **Further Along** tape.

86. Thomas Moore **Care of the Soul** (New York: HarperPerennial, 1992), 58-71.

87. W. Grant Dahlstrom, George Schlager Welsh, and Leona E. Dahlstrom **An MMPI Handbook**, Revised Edition, Vol 1 Clinical Interpretation (Minneapolis: University of Minnesota Press, 1972).

88. Rogers, 133.

89. ibid, 140.

90. ibid. 143.

91. Stephen Covey **Living the Seven Habits, Applications and Insights** (Nightengale-Conant Tape Series, 1991).

92. Rogers, 154.

Chapter 17

93. Maslow

94. Leo Buscalia **Personhood: The Art of Being Fully Human** (New York: Fawcett Columbine, 1982).

95. Jim Simkin, (Patient-Model Gestalt Therapy Training Program, Esalen, California, 1976).

96. Shirley Maclaine **Out On A Limb** (New York: Bantam Books, 1983).

97. Brian Weiss **Many Lives, Many Masters** (New York: Simon & Schuster, 1988)

98. John F. Thie **Touch For Health** (Marina del Rey, California: DeVorss, 1973, 1994).

99. Maslow

Chapter 18

100. Tony Robbins **Unlimited Power** (Nightingale-Conant Tape Series, 1989).

101. Morris, 53.

102. Barry Neil Kaufman **To Love is To Be Happy With** (New York: Fawcett, Columbine, 1977), 65.

103. ibid, 63.

104. Mary Edwards Wertsch **Military Brats, Legacies of Childhood Inside the Fortress** (New York: Macmillan, 1991) 26-27.

Chapter 19

105. Bradshaw

106. Whitfield

107. Louise Hay **The Power Is Within You** (Santa Monica: Hay House, Inc., 1991).

108. Susan Forward **Toxic Parents: Overcoming Their Hurtful Legacy and Reclaiming Your Life** (New York: Bantam Books,1989), 187.

Chapter 20

109. ibid, 188.

Chapter 22

110. Hay

111. Topping

REFERENCES

Arrien, Angeles (1990) "Four Basic Archetypal Ways Found in Shamanic Traditions," **Revisions**. Fall.

Balint, Michael (1968) **The Basic Fault**. London: Tavistock Publications, pp. 59-73.

Bass, Ellen and Davis, Laura (1988). **Courage To Heal**. New York: Harper & Row.

Bernard, Michael E. (1991) **Procrastinate Later.** Australia: Schwartz & Wilkinson.

Bettelheim, Bruno (1960) **The Informed Heart: Autonomy in a Mass Age**. New York: Macmillan, Free Press. pp. 447-449.

Bradshaw, John (1968) **Bradshaw On The Family.** Pompano Beach, Florida: Health Communications.

---- (1988) **Healing the Shame That Binds You.** New York: Bantam Books.

---- (1990) **Homecoming: Reclaiming and Championing Your Inner Child.** New York: Bantam Books.

Brandon, Nathanial (1969) **The Psychology of Self-Esteem**. New York: Bantam Books.

Burka, Jane B. & Yuen, Lenora (1983) **Procrastination.** Reading, Massachusetts; Menlo Park, California: Addison-Wesley.

Buscalia, Leo (1982) **Personhood: The Art of Being Fully Human.** New York: Fawcett Columbine.

Carter, Steve (1987) **Men Who Can't Love. When A Man's Fear Makes Him Run From Commitment**. New York: M. Evans and Co.

Chopra, Deepak (1987) **Creating Health**. Boston: Houghton Mifflin.

---- (1989) **Quantum Healing**. New York: Bantam Books.

---- (1991, 1992) **Unconditional Life: Mastering the Forces That Shape Personal Reality.** New York: Bantam Books.

---- (1990) **Magical Mind, Magical Body.** Chicago: Nightingale-Conant Corporation Tape Series.

Cohen, Alan (1981) **The Dragon Doesn't Live Here Any More.** Kula, Hawaii: Alan Cohen Publications and Workshops.

Coleman, James C. (1964) **Abnormal Psychology and Modern Life. Third Edition**. Illinois: Scott, Foreman and Company.

Covey, Stephan R. (1993) **Living the Seven Habits**. Covey Leadership Center Tape Series.

---- (1989) **The Seven Habits of Highly Effective People.** New York: Simon & Schuster.

Dahlstrom, W. Grant, Welsh, George Schlager, and Dahlstrom, Leona E. (1960, 1972, 1979) **An MMPI Handbook** Vol 1, Clinical Interpretation. Minneapolis: University of Minnesota.

Dewe, Bruce (1990). **Sabotage Programmes. Professional Kinesiology Training Programs.** Switzerland: International Kinesiology College.

Dyer, Wayne (1989) **You'll See It When You Believe It**. New York: W. Morrow.

---- (1987) **Transformations**. Chicago: Nightingale-Conant Corporation Tape Series.

----(1992) **Real Magic**. Chicago: Nightingale-Conant Corporation Tape Series.

Emery, Gary (1982) **Own Your Own Life.** New York: New American Library.

Emery, Stewart (1978) **Actualizations: You Don't Have to Rehearse to Be Yourself.** New York: Doubleday & Company, Inc.

Erikson, E.H. (1963) **Childhood and Society.** New York: W.W. Norton & Company.

---- (1968) **Identity, Youth and Crisis**. New York: W.W. Norton & Co. Inc.

---- (1956) "The Problem of Ego Identity", **Journal of American Psychoanalytic Association**. Vol.IV, pp. 56-121.

Farber, Adele and Mazish, Elaine (1987) **Siblings Without Rivilry**. New York: W. W. Norton and Co.

Forward, Susan (1989). **Toxic Parents: Overcoming Their Hurtful Legacy and Reclaiming Your Life.** New York: Bantam Books.

Freedman, Alfred M. and Kaplan, Harold I. and Sadock, Benjamin J. (1975) **Comprehensive Textbook of Psychiatry/I. Second Edition.** Baltimore: The Williams and Wilkins Company.

Freud, Sigmund (1939) **Moses and Monotheism**. London: Hogarth Press.

Frankl, Victor (1971) **Man's Search For Meaning**. New York: Washington Square Press.

Erich Fromm (1973) **The Anatomy of Human Destructiveness.** Connecticut: Fawcett Publications, Inc.

Glasser, William (1965) **Reality Therapy.** New York: Harper & Row.

Gordon, Thomas (1970) **Parent Effectiveness Training.** New York: Peter H. Wyden, Inc.

Hammer, Emanuel E. (Ed.) (1968) **The Use of Interpretation in Treatment.** New York: Grune and Stratton.

Hartmann, Heintz (1958) **Ego Psychology and the Problem of Adaptation.** New York: International Universities Press, Inc.

Hay, Louise (1982) **Heal Your Body.** Santa Monica, California: Hay House, Inc.

---- (1991) **Power is Within.** Santa Monica, California. Hay House, Inc.

Hedges, Lawrence (1983) **Listening Perspectives in Psychotherapy.** New York: Jason Aronson.

Hedges, Lawrence and Hulgas, Joyce (1991) **Working the Organizing Experience.** Video Tape. Orange County Psychoanalytic Institute.

Hinsie, L.E. and Campbell, R.J. (1960) **Psychiatric Dictionary.** 3rd Edition. New York: Oxford University Press.

Hopkins, Nancy Myer "Symbolic Church Fights." **Congregations.** May/June 1993.

Jacobson, Edith (1954) **The Self and the Object World: Vicissitudes of their Infantile Cathexis and Their Influence of Ideational and Affective Development."** The Psychoanalytic Study of the Child. New York: International Universities Press.

Joekel, Nancy (1978) "The Question of Choice." **Touch For Health Journal**. Pasadena, California: Touch For Health Foundation.

John-Roger and McWilliams, Peter (1991) **Life 101. You Can't Afford the Luxury of a Negative Thought.** Los Angeles: Prelude Press.

---- (1991) **Do It! Let's Get Off Our Butts**. Los Angeles: Prelude Press.

Johnson, Kerry (1990) **The Science of Self-Discipline**. Chicago: Nightingale-Conant Corporation Tape Series.

Jung, Carl (1923) **Psychological Types**. New York: Harcourt Brace.

Justice, Blair (1988) **Who Gets Sick** Los Angeles: J.P. Tarcher.

Kaufman, Barry Neil (1977) **To Love is to Be Happy With**. New York: Fawcett Columbine.

Keirsey, David and Bates, Marilyn (1984) **Please Understand Me**. Del Mar, California: Prometheus Nemesis Book Company.

Kohut, Heintz (1978) **The Search For the Self.** Ed. Paul H. Orenstein. New York: International Universities Press, Inc.

Kovacs, Arthur (1968) "Ego Psychology and Self Theory" in Buhler, Charlotte and Massarek, F. **The Course of Human Life.** New York: Springer.

Kovel, Joel, A. (1976) **A Complete Guide to Therapy**. New York: Pantheon Books.

Kubler-Ross, E. (1969) **On Death and Dying.** New York: Macmillan.

Luft, J. & Ingham, H. (1961) **The Johari Window, A Graphic Model for Interpersonal Relations**, Western Training Laboratory in Group Development, August 1955; University of California at Los Angeles,

Extension Office. See Also: Human Relations Training News. Washington D.C.: National Education Association. V. No. 1.

Luft, Joseph (1963) **Group Processes, An Introduction to Group Dynamics,** The National Press.

Lumet, Sidney. Television Interview.

MacLaine, Shirley (1991) **Dance While You Can.** New York: Bantam Books.

---- (1983) **Out on a Limb**. New York: Bantam.

Mahler, M.S. (1968) **On Human Symbiosis and the Vicissitudes of Individuation.** New York: International Universities Press.

Maslow, Abraham (1968). **Toward A Psychology of Being.** Princeton, New Jersey: Van Nostrand.

May, Rollo (1981) **Freedom & Destiny**, New York: Norton.

McKay, Matthew, David, Martha, Fanning, Patrick. (1983) **Messages. The Communications Skills Book.** Oakland, California: New Harbinger Publications.

Miller, Alice (1983) **The Drama of the Gifted Child.** New York: Harper.

---- (1984) **Thou Shalt Not Be Aware. Society's Betrayal of the Child**. New York: New American Library.

---- (1983) **For Your Own Good. Hidden Cruelty in Child-Rearing**. New York: Farrar, Straus, Giroux.

Montagu, Ashley (1971) **The Elephant Man, A Study of Human Dignity**. New York: Ballantine Books.

Moore, Thomas (1992) **Care Of The Soul.** New York: Harper Perennial.

Morris, William (1982) **American Heritage Dictionary**. Boston: Houghton Mifflin.

Murray, Henry. Quote from John-Roger, McWilliams, Peter, Boyer, Tom (1989) **You Can't Afford the Luxury of a Negative Thought.** Los Angeles, California: Prelude Press

Myers, Isabel Briggs (1982) **Introduction To Type**. Third Edition. Palo Alto, California: Consulting Psychologists Press, Inc.

Namka, Lynne (1989) **Doormat Syndrome**. Florida: Health Communications, Inc.

Nebel, Gene (1980) Notes from lecture given to New Jersey's Department of Human Services on **Ego Psychology.**

O'Connor, Lynn E. (1993) "Control Mastery Theory and the Treatment of the Addict." **California Psychologist**. Jan.

O'Connor, Lynn E. and Weiss, Joseph (1993) "Individual Psychotherapy for Addicted Clients: An Application of Control Mastery Theory." **Journal of Psychoactive Drugs**. Oct-Dec.

Oleska, Paula. (1992) "Emotional Integration." **Touch For Health Journal.** Pasadena, California: Touch For Health Association.

Pearson, Gerald H. J. Editor (1968) **Handbook of Child Psychoanalysis**. New York: Basic Books.

Pease, Jeffery (1993) "Exercising Your Emotional Options" **Body, Mind & Spirit.** March/April.

Peck, M. Scott (1993) **Applications on Further Along The Road Less Travelled**. Chicago: Nightingale-Conant Corporation.

---- (1992) **Further Along The Road Less Travelled.** New York: Simon & Schuster

---- (1983) **People of the Lie.** New York: Simon & Schuster, Inc.

---- (1978) **The Road Less Travelled.** New York: Simon & Schuster.

Perls, Frederick (1969) Lecture at Esalen Institute.

Pillari, Vimala (1991) **Scapegoating in Families. Intergenerational Patterns of Physical and Emotional Abuse**. New York: Brunner/Mazel.

Powell, John (1969) **Why Am I Afraid To Tell You Who I Am?** Valencia, California: Tabor Publishing.

Rainwater, Janette (1979) **You're In Charge.** Marina del Rey: DeVorss.

Redfield, James (1993) **The Celestine Prophecy.** New York: Warner Books.

Robbins, Tony (1989) **Unlimited Power.** Chicago: Nightingale-Conant Tape Series.

Roche, Suski. Founder of First Zen Center in the U.S.

Rogers, C.R. (1961) **On Becoming A Person.** Boston: Houghton Mifflin Company.

Rosenberg, Jack (1989) **Body, Self, & Soul: Sustaining Integration.** Georgia: Humanics New Age.

Searles, Harold F. (1986) **My Work With Borderline Patients.** Northvale, New Jersey. Jason Aronson, Inc.

Schaef, Anne Wilson (1986) **Co-Dependence: Misunderstood-- Mistreated.** Cambridge: Harper & Row.

Siegel, Bernie (1986) **Love, Medicine, and Miracles.** New York: Harper & Row, Publishers.

Smedes, Lewis B. (1993) **Shame and Grace. Healing the Shame We Don't Deserve**. San Francisco, California: Harper.

Spitz, Renee. In Freud, Anna. (1946) "Anaclitic Depression," **The Psychoanalytic Study of the Child**. Vol 2. Eds. Eissler, H. Freud, A. Hartman, H. Kris, E. New York: International Universities Press.

Stokes, G. and Whiteside, D. (1989) **Structural Neurology.** Burbank, California: Three In One Concepts Publication.

Stolorow Robert, and Atwood, George (1993) **Organizing Principle.** (paper)

Thie, John F. (1973, 1994) **Touch For Health.** Santa Monica, California: DeVorss.

Topping, Wayne (1987, 1992) **What Makes You Tick, Makes You Sick.** Bellingham, Washington: Topping International Institute.

Tracy, Brian (1989) **How To Master Your Time.** Chicago: Nightingale-Conant Tape Series.

Waitley, Denis (1991) **The Psychology of Human Motivation.** Chicago: Nightingale-Conant Corporation Tape Series.

Webster's Dictionary of English Usage (1989) Springfield, Massachusetts: Merriam-Webster.

Weiss, Brian L. (1988) **Many Lives, Many Masters**. New York: Simon & Schuster.

Wertsch, Mary Edwards (1991) **Military Brats, Legacies of Childhood Inside the Fortress.** New York: Harmony Books.

Whitfield, Charles L. (1987). **Healing the Child Within.** Florida: Health Communications, Inc.

Whitfield, Charles L. Workshop on **Healing the Child Within.** 1990

Wickett, Mike (1987) **It's All Within Your Reach**. Nightengale-Conant Corporation Tape Series.

Wilds, Stuart (1987). **Life Was Never Meant To Be A Struggle**. Taos, New Mexico: White Dove International, Inc., p.2.

Winnicott, D.W. (1956). "Primary Maternal Preoccupation." pp. 300-305 in **Through Paediatrics to Psych-Analysis.** New York: Basic Books, pp. 300-305.

---- (1972, 1986) **Holding and Interpretation**. New York: Grove Press.

Yalom, Irvin (1975) **Theory and Practice of Group Psychotherapy.** New York: Basic Books.

Zasloff, David (1992) Tee Shirt saying originator.

Zukav, Gary (1979) **The Dancing Wu Li Masters**. New York: Bantam Books.